THE MULTI-COOKER
BABY FOOD COOKBOOK

The MULTI-COOKER BABY·FOOD COOKBOOK

100 EASY RECIPES FOR YOUR SLOW COOKER, PRESSURE COOKER, OR MULTI-COOKER

jenna helwig

with

Toby Amidor, MS, RD, CDN

HOUGHTON MIFFLIN HARCOURT | BOSTON NEW YORK 2019

For information about permission to reproduce selections
from this book, write to trade.permissions@hmhco.com or to
Permissions, Houghton Mifflin Harcourt Publishing Company, 3
Park Avenue, 19th Floor, New York, New York 10016.

hmhbooks.com

Library of Congress Cataloging-in-Publication Data

Names: Helwig, Jenna, author. | Amidor, Toby, author.
Title: The multi-cooker baby food cookbook : 100 easy recipes
for your slow cooker, pressure cooker, or multi-cooker / Jenna
Helwig with Toby Amidor, MS, RD, CDN.
Description: Boston : Houghton Mifflin Harcourt, 2019. | Includes
index.
Identifiers: LCCN 2019013134 (print) | LCCN 2019013932
(ebook) | ISBN 9780358105572 (ebook) | ISBN 9780358108573
(trade paper)
Subjects: LCSH: Electric cooking, Slow. | Pressure cooking. |
Baby foods. | LCGFT: Cookbooks.
Classification: LCC TX827 (ebook) | LCC TX827 .H3895 2019
(print) | DDC
641.5/884—dc23
LC record available at https://lccn.loc.
gov/2019013134

Book design by Alissa Faden

Printed in China

SCP 10 9 8 7 6 5 4 3 2 1

For R, forever

contents

YOU CAN MAKE YOUR OWN BABY FOOD

!★!★!★!★!

introduction

YOU CAN MAKE YOUR OWN BABY FOOD—REALLY—and using a multi-cooker or slow cooker is an easy and convenient way to do it.

Yes, I know you're up to your ears in dirty diapers and maybe your little one isn't quite sleeping through the night yet. (Soon, I promise.)

If you weren't a cook before, making baby food is the ideal way to get your feet wet. The ingredient list is usually short and the method uncomplicated. And using your multi-cooker means the whole process is even easier.

If you're already a cook, but are dubious about the Instant Pot and similar appliances—a.k.a. multi-cookers—I understand. I've been there. I was skeptical about giving up precious counter space to another bulky appliance. But once I tried it, I was an instant (pun intended) convert. My multi-cooker gave me the gift of time by letting me put my food in the pot, set the cook time, and walk away. No stirring and no checking required. Plus, the food tastes good. In fact, sometimes better than it would have if made on the stovetop.

If you've already joined the cult of the Instant Pot (or a similar appliance), then I really don't need to convince you of anything! You know that these handy devices can make your kitchen life much easier. But you might still be asking why you should bother making your own baby food, and why the multi-cooker is the best tool for the job.

THE BENEFITS OF MAKING HOMEMADE BABY FOOD IN THE MULTI-COOKER

YOU'RE IN CONTROL. When you make your own baby food, you're not limited by the varieties on the supermarket shelves. You choose the foods, the flavors, and the textures. You can customize everything for *your* baby.

YOU CAN WALK AWAY. The biggest benefit to cooking with a multi-cooker (or slow cooker) is that once the food is in the pot and the lid is sealed, you're done! When pressure-cooking using a multi-cooker, not everything is super-speedy, since it takes time for the cooker to come up to pressure and then release pressure at the end. But you don't have to stand by the stove—there's no stirring, no flipping, and no monitoring liquid levels. The machine is doing the work for you, so you can spend more time on other tasks (or playing with your baby).

IT'S EASY. When you use a multi-cooker, preparing homemade baby food is simpler than ever. Most recipes require only one pot, and if you use an immersion blender, there are no messy transfers to a food processor or standard blender. That means fewer dishes to wash and less fuss.

IT'S ECONOMICAL. Turning four apples into 2½ cups of applesauce is less expensive than buying the equivalent amount of apple purée baby food. And homemade applesauce tastes better, too.

YOUR BABY CAN EAT WHAT YOU EAT. Your baby can join you at the family table sooner than you may think. When you prepare meals with the whole family in mind, your baby becomes an independent eater more quickly. The family recipes in chapter four will get you started. Each recipe is appropriate for most babies eight months and up, but has flavors that everyone else at the table is craving.

KEEP IN MIND, TOO, THAT IT ISN'T ALL OR NOTHING. Being a new parent is hard, and sometimes preparing all your baby's food from scratch just isn't in the cards. It is 100% okay to mix and match between homemade and store-bought food. My goal with this book (and my previous books, *Real Baby Food* and *Baby-Led Feeding*) is to arm you with information and recipes so you can make smart choices about feeding your family, but also have fun during the process. So let's get cooking!

YOU'RE
IN
CONTROL

IT'S EASY

YOU CAN
WALK AWAY

IT'S
ECONOMICAL

MULTI-COOKERS
ARE THE NEW BABY
FOOD MAKERS

YOUR BABY
CAN EAT
WHAT YOU EAT

IT ISN'T
ALL OR
NOTHING

HOW TO USE THIS BOOK

CHAPTER ONE offers the building blocks of feeding your baby: when to start, how to start, and what to start with, plus helpful information on portion sizes and how to put together a balanced meal plan. We'll take a deeper dive into nutrition here as well, highlighting some of the important nutrients for babies and where to find them. This chapter also addresses food allergies and gives advice on preventing them.

CHAPTER TWO features single-ingredient purées and finger foods appropriate for beginning eaters. They range from the traditional (think sweet potatoes and pears) to the unexpected (rutabaga and eggplant, for example). These recipes highlight what a multi-cooker does best: taking hard foods and cooking them quickly so they're a silky-soft texture that just happens to be perfect for a baby. Plus, I explain how to take advantage of a multi-cooker's ability to make yogurt and hard-boiled eggs, two excellent foods for beginning eaters.

The recipes in **CHAPTER THREE** are for babies ready for more texture and mixed foods. There are still some dishes to be spoon-fed or offered to your baby on a preloaded spoon, including Sesame Pears (page 100) and Go Green Purée (page 97). But many foods, like Tropical Fruit Salad (page 107) and Blueberry Banana Bread (page 119), are ideal for self-feeding. Some of these recipes, such as Broccoli Patties (page 130) and Get-Your-Greens Quinoa Bites (page 125), begin in the multi-cooker but are finished on the stovetop or in the oven to introduce other textures.

CHAPTER FOUR is all about eating together as a family. These dishes are appropriate for babies—not too salty, not too spicy, and soft enough to eat safely—but satisfying for bigger kids and adults. This isn't "baby food," but family food that babies can enjoy, too. Some of my favorites include Mexican-Style Mash Bowls (page 162), Lemon-Dill Salmon (page 206), and Every Bean Soup (page 199).

ABOUT THE RECIPE ICONS

 FREEZER FRIENDLY These recipes are ideal to make ahead or double up on so you can freeze them now and take advantage of them later. Most foods are best defrosted overnight in the fridge, but the microwave can often be used in a pinch.

 FINGER FOOD These recipes, or variations on these recipes, are finger foods perfect for self-feeding babies, whether you're also including purées in the mix or exclusively practicing baby-led feeding.

30 MINUTES OR LESS These recipes are ready in a half hour or less, start to finish, including the time it takes the multi-cooker to come up to pressure.

Nutrition Numbers for Babies 6 to 12 Months

All the recipes in this book include nutrition information. My goal isn't to have you count calories or tally up milligrams of iron. But it is helpful to have a general idea of how your baby is eating over the course of a week or so. Remember, your little one is still getting the bulk of her nutrition from breastmilk or formula, so don't worry if she isn't hitting these benchmarks on a daily basis.

Calories	600-900
Protein	11 grams
Calcium	260 milligrams
Iron	11 milligrams
Potassium	700 milligrams
Vitamin C	50 milligrams
Vitamin A	2,000 IU

CHAPTER ONE
RAISING A HAPPY,
HEALTHY
EATER

WHEN
TO
START

If you've Googled "When to start solids," you've probably seen a lot of inconsistent advice. The World Health Organization (WHO) and American Academy of Pediatrics (AAP) recommend exclusive breastfeeding until six months, but don't address when formula-fed babies should start solid foods. The American Academy of Allergy, Asthma, and Immunology (AAAAI) recommends that babies begin eating common allergens between the ages of four and six months to help prevent food allergies, and many pediatricians continue to recommend starting between four and six months. To make matters more confusing, a recent study from the Centers for Disease Control and Prevention (CDC) reported that 16 percent of American babies started solids before four months.

Whew! So what's the real story?

The easy part is this: do not offer your baby solids before four months. It provides no benefit and can in fact cause harm, raising the risk of choking. Babies this young are perfectly nourished by breastmilk or formula.

After four months, the rules are less clear-cut. But the good news is that you only need to worry about one person when you are deciding when to introduce solid foods—your baby. Babies develop at different rates; here are some signs that your baby is ready to start eating solid foods:

▶ Your baby can sit up with light support; think rolled-up dish towels in the high chair.

▶ She has good head control.

▶ Your baby has lost the tongue-thrust reflex that automatically pushes food (or anything else) out of her mouth.

▶ She watches avidly while you eat and reaches for your food or fork.

There is nothing official about this, but chances are, you'll know when your baby is ready. I could just tell that my daughter was *hungry* when she was almost six months old; her liquid diet wasn't satisfying her anymore. She was ready for the fun and nourishment that come with solid foods.

Most babies are ready between five and six months. If you want to skip purées and start exclusively with finger foods (see more about baby-led weaning on page 76), waiting until closer to six months is usually best, since younger babies have a harder time self-feeding and may become frustrated . . . and hungry!

On the flip side, if your baby is developmentally ready for solids, don't delay too long or you'll lose valuable time taste training and exposing your baby to allergens. By seven months most babies should be experimenting with solid foods.

HOW TO START

It's time! Here's how to ensure that your baby's first experiences with solid foods are positive.

▶ Make sure he's sitting up in a high chair or baby chair. It's okay if you have to use some rolled-up dish towels for extra support.

▶ Give your baby his first bites in the morning. That way you'll have the whole day to monitor for allergic reactions.

▶ Offer your baby food when he's alert and happy. A grouchy, sleepy baby usually doesn't have much patience for solid foods.

▶ You also want your baby to be in the comfortable in-between place of hungry and satisfied when you start. If he's too hungry, he may become frustrated when he can't eat quickly enough to satiate himself. If he's too full, he won't be interested in eating more. Consider offering your baby his first foods about an hour after breastfeeding or formula-feeding.

▶ Whether you're spoon-feeding or offering your baby safe finger foods, let him touch and explore the food. Eating is about more than just nutrition and taste.

▶ Only offer food as long as your baby is interested. If he closes his mouth, seems distracted, or pushes away the spoon, move on. Don't worry if he hasn't eaten a full serving. We want our babies to become attuned to their hunger levels and not eat beyond fullness.

▶ Nix any distractions at the high chair. No phones or videos, although a little relaxing music is okay.

▶ Always stay with your baby when he's eating.

what exactly are "solid foods"?

Even the words *solid foods* can seem confusing. In this case, it means any food that isn't formula or breastmilk, from finger foods to purées . . . even if a purée doesn't actually seem *solid*. Another term you might see is *complementary foods*, which means foods to complement—that is, accompany—breastmilk or formula. It's all the same thing, and just means the real food you're adding to your baby's diet in addition to breastmilk or formula.

WHAT TO START WITH

Pediatricians used to recommend starting with rice cereal, because it was fortified with essential nutrients, easy to digest, and bland. These days we know that bland is not a perk when it comes to feeding babies. We want our little ones to experience big flavor right from the start. So while baby cereal is still an okay option, you have lots of other choices.

In fact, what you decide to start with is virtually limitless. Start with a vegetable or fruit, and no, there's no evidence that if babies start eating fruit first, they'll shun veggies later. Or start with meat for a boost of essential minerals like zinc or iron.

You should, however, start with one food at a time for at least the first few weeks of feeding. If your baby has an allergic reaction to anything, this will help you isolate which food is the culprit. Until you have a good handle on your baby's tolerances, wait a day between introducing new foods. The traditional advice is to wait three to five days between offering new foods to monitor for allergic reactions, but I, and many other experts, believe this is excessive. Most reactions are apparent within a day, and waiting so long between offering new foods means you'll lose valuable time introducing a variety of flavors. As with most everything, when it comes to feeding your baby, it's up to you!

If you're starting with a purée, thin it out with a little water, breastmilk, or formula if it seems too thick. If you're starting with a finger food, make sure it's soft and appropriately sized (see page 76).

forbidden foods

Don't feed your baby honey or any food containing honey until age one, since honey can be tainted with botulism. Also avoid choking hazards such as popcorn, whole nuts, gobs of nut butter, hot dogs, hard foods, and whole grapes. Cow's milk is a no-no as a primary drink (stick with breastmilk or formula) because it can be hard to digest. But cheese and yogurt are okay, and it's fine to use some milk in cooking your baby's foods.

WHEN TO FEED YOUR BABY

A baby's eating schedule can be annoyingly out of whack with the rest of the family's. (Really, dinner at five p.m.?) It can be unrealistic to actually eat with your baby every meal of the day, but try to get in the habit of eating together as often as possible. Maybe you eat breakfast together or lunch on the weekends. The key is for your baby to see you enjoying real, healthy food.

Your baby watching you eat a kale salad doesn't mean he's going to magically love leafy greens, but vegetables and other healthy foods will be a normal part of the daily routine. He will see how you use a fork and a napkin, and that it's okay to stop eating when you're full. You are your baby's most important teacher, and actions speak louder than words.

And sooner rather than later, try to eat the same thing at the same time. This will likely happen sooner if your baby is practicing baby-led weaning (eating finger foods right from the start; see page 76), or if you're prepping the family meals in chapter four of this book.

YOU ARE YOUR BABY'S MOST IMPORTANT TEACHER, AND ACTIONS SPEAK LOUDER THAN WORDS.

does your baby need a supplement?

Many parents wonder whether supplements are necessary for their baby to get all the nourishment needed for proper growth and development. As with so many things when it comes to feeding babies, the answer is, "It depends." Speak with your pediatrician before starting any supplements.

COOKING EQUIPMENT

Multi-Cooker

The recipes in this book were tested using an Instant Pot Duo 60, an Instant Pot Duo 60 V2, and a Fagor LUX 6-quart multi-cooker, but any 6-quart electric pressure cooker or multi-cooker will do the job. (Note that Fagor brand multi-cookers are now sold under the name Zavor.) A stovetop pressure cooker cooks at higher pressure, so recipes made in these appliances should take less time. But since the instructions in this book pertain only to electric models, if you want to use a stovetop model, you'll have to experiment to get to know your appliance.

Multi-cookers have numerous different cooking functions, including high-pressure cooking, yogurt-making, slow-cooking, and settings like "poultry," "bean," and "meat." Most of the recipes in this book use the high-pressure-cooking function since that's what makes a multi-cooker so amazing—cooking foods fast in a superhot, high-pressure environment.

GET TO KNOW YOUR APPLIANCE ⇨

Regardless of which multi-cooker you use, be sure to read the manual. These appliances aren't always intuitive to operate at first, but once you cook a few recipes, you'll get the hang of it.

Slow Cooker

About half the recipes in this book feature directions for preparing the dish in a slow cooker instead of a multi-cooker. The instructions are tailored to a stand-alone, 4-quart (unless otherwise noted) slow cooker, not the Slow Cook function on a multi-cooker.

Blenders

One of the best parts about making baby food in a multi-cooker or slow cooker is that with an immersion blender, you can make purées right in the pot. But the immersion blender you use makes a big difference. If the motor isn't strong enough, it can take an awfully long time to purée a bunch of, say, green beans. I have been happy with my All-Clad stainless steel immersion blender. An immersion blender works especially well for very soft foods like squash, apples, or even meat. It's also good for when you want your baby's food to have a little more texture.

If you're looking for a perfectly smooth purée, a standard blender is your best bet, even though it means you will have to transfer foods out of the pot (and wash more dishes!). If you're having a hard time getting a smooth purée with an immersion

blender or standard blender, add a little water to loosen up the ingredients.

Potato Masher

This classic kitchen tool is one of my favorites to use for making baby food. With a little elbow grease, it makes quick work of many foods, and it's easy to use right inside the multi-cooker pot.

Steamers

Don't overlook the flat metal rack that came with your multi-cooker. It acts as a steamer, allowing foods or dishes to sit above the water in the pot. The flat rack is ideal for larger foods like halved spaghetti squash. It also makes a handy inside-the-pot trivet for holding cooking vessels containing stratas, breads, and frittatas. For smaller foods like chopped fruit or vegetables, I prefer to employ the same metal steamer basket that I use in a pot for steaming on the stovetop.

Soufflé Dish

Speaking of stratas, breads, and frittatas, to make these you'll need a 1½-quart round stoneware soufflé dish. Happily, a dish of this size also comes in handy as a serving bowl or a baking dish, so it won't be a multi-cooker-only purchase.

Sling

When you cook with a soufflé dish in the multi-cooker, you won't be able to reach in with potholder-ed hands to remove it. One workaround

is to fashion a sling out of aluminum foil. Cut a sheet of foil about 20 inches long. Fold it into thirds lengthwise like a letter. Place the sling under the soufflé dish and use the excess foil on either side as handles. Another option—and my preference—is to use a silicone sling created especially for pressure cookers. I love the OXO Good Grips Pressure Cooker Sling.

Candy Thermometer

If you plan on making yogurt in the multi-cooker, a candy thermometer will take a lot of the guesswork out of the process.

Other than that, you'll just need basic kitchenware to prep food for the multi-cooker, or to finish up recipes on the stove or in the oven, including:

- A large cutting board (trust me, you'll feel instantly more organized if you aren't chopping everything on a small board)

- Two baking sheets
- Chef's knife (keep this sharp!)
- Paring knife
- Serrated bread knife
- Whisk
- Kitchen shears
- Spatula
- Tongs
- Ladle
- 1 or 2 wooden spoons
- 1 or 2 rubber spatulas
- Various pots and pans
- Small and large mixing bowls
- Box grater
- Mini-muffin tins
- Measuring cups and spoons
- Vegetable peeler
- Microplane grater

MULTI-COOKER TIPS, TRICKS, AND REMINDERS

▶ Read your manual! Yes, I know this isn't the most exciting advice, but models vary, and at least skimming the instructions really will help you navigate your appliance.

▶ Food that has been cooked under pressure is VERY HOT. Take cooling time into account when you're planning your meal.

▶ Unlike on the stovetop, where you can turn the heat down a touch, depending on your model of multi-cooker you have little or no control over the temperature when cooking on the Sauté setting. If your food is browning too quickly, there are a few things you can do: add a little more oil to the pot, add a tablespoon or more of water, or turn off the multi-cooker for a minute or two. The residual heat means your food will continue cooking. Once the sizzling really slows down, you can hit Sauté again to finish up.

▶ Cooking times vary depending on numerous factors, including how small a vegetable has been chopped, how old your dried beans are, and exactly how much liquid is in the pot. I prefer to err on the low end of the cooking time to start because you can always reseal the pot and cook for another minute or two or more.

▶ If you are trying to reseal the pot, because the recipe specified doing so or because you want to cook your food a bit longer, remember that you won't be able to reseal the lid right away. The contents of the pot will be too hot for the lid to lock on securely with the pressure valve down. Wait about five minutes and you should be good to go. The pot will come up to pressure more quickly than when you began cooking since the contents are already hot.

FOOD THAT HAS BEEN COOKED UNDER PRESSURE IS VERY HOT

COOKING IN BULK

Preparing your own baby food in a multi-cooker means you can make large batches. The food can be frozen and defrosted on an as-needed basis. Since babies eat such small quantities, you could conceivably make enough food for the month in just a couple of hours on a Sunday. Here are some things to keep in mind.

▶ Purées, soups, stews, and most saucy things freeze well. So do pancakes, patties, meatballs, and baked goods. What doesn't like the deep freeze? Anything with very little liquid, such as plain cooked meats, poultry, or fish. For example, chicken meatballs freeze well, but cooked chicken breasts, not so much. Recipes in this book that freeze well are marked with the snowflake icon.

▶ Before freezing, divide purées into small portions. Spoon them into ice cube trays or special baby-food freezer containers. Freeze, and if using ice cube trays, transfer the frozen cubes to a large container or zip-top bag. Make sure to label everything with the type of food and the date.

▶ To defrost, place an individual serving in the refrigerator overnight. Yes, this requires a bit of advance planning! Make it a habit each evening to think about what your baby will eat the next day and defrost what you need. If you're in a jam, it's okay to defrost purées on the stovetop or in the microwave. Just be sure the food is barely warm or at room temperature before offering it to your baby.

▶ The same goes for family meals. Place the frozen soup, stew, or casserole in the fridge one or two days before you plan to serve it. If you need to finish the defrosting in the microwave or on the stovetop, it shouldn't take long. Never leave food on the counter for more than two hours to defrost.

SAFETY FIRST! KEEP BABY FOOD IN THE FRIDGE FOR UP TO THREE DAYS AND IN THE FREEZER FOR UP TO THREE MONTHS.

should you buy organic?

For many parents, buying organic foods for their babies is a foregone conclusion, but the issue isn't black and white. Organic foods can be significantly more expensive than their conventional counterparts, and for those of us on a budget, buying nonorganic foods can cause serious guilt. You have probably seen posts and stories on social media calling nonorganic foods toxic, a shot at the heart of concerned parents.

Conventionally grown foods are not toxic. The federal government sets strict limits for the amount of pesticide residues foods can harbor. Even the foods on the Environmental Working Group's "Dirty Dozen" list do not meet these thresholds. Now, many people—some scientists included—believe that the federal government's pesticide limits are too high. But virtually all experts agree it is vitally important for people—including babies!—to eat an abundance of fruits and vegetables, organic or not. Yes, conventional strawberries do likely harbor more pesticide residue than organically grown strawberries. If you can afford the organic without impacting other healthy items on your grocery list, go for it.

But if your choice is between conventional strawberries or no strawberries, go for the conventional strawberries. Wash them well and watch your baby enjoy. I promise you are not poisoning your child.

In the end, buying organic or not is a personal choice based on a variety of factors. In my house, I buy organic eggs and milk, and pork and chicken that have been raised without antibiotics. I'll purchase organic fruits and veggies when they're on sale, or if they're only a bit more expensive than the conventional version. Even better, I like to get my produce at the local farmers' market. Not all the foods there are organic, but they have been grown nearby, in season, by people in my wider community. That, I'll spend a few more dollars for.

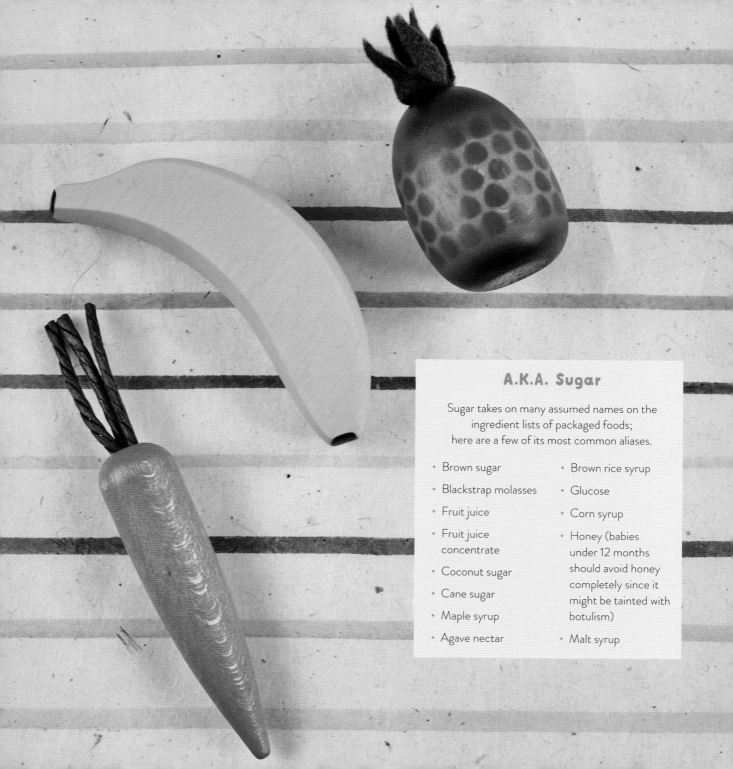

A.K.A. Sugar

Sugar takes on many assumed names on the
ingredient lists of packaged foods;
here are a few of its most common aliases.

- Brown sugar
- Blackstrap molasses
- Fruit juice
- Fruit juice concentrate
- Coconut sugar
- Cane sugar
- Maple syrup
- Agave nectar

- Brown rice syrup
- Glucose
- Corn syrup
- Honey (babies under 12 months should avoid honey completely since it might be tainted with botulism)
- Malt syrup

SALT AND SUGAR

SALT: Babies' kidneys have a hard time processing sodium, so avoid adding salt to your child's food during his first year of life. It's okay if there is natural sodium in the food (such as from shrimp), or if a little sneaks in from low-sodium broths or canned beans. If your baby is eating table food with the rest of the family, consider reducing the amount of salt called for in the recipe or omitting it altogether and letting grown-ups and bigger kids add salt at the table.

The recipes in chapters two and three don't include any salt. I do include salt as an optional ingredient in the family meals in chapter four. My hope is that you will continue to use these recipes after your baby is 12 months old; at that point, you'll likely want to include salt for maximum deliciousness.

When you do use salt in recipes, opt for kosher or sea salt, since they have less sodium than table salt and a cleaner, less chemical taste. Having a flaky sea salt on hand for finishing a dish, almost as a garnish, is also an easy way to boost the flavor of what you're cooking. My favorite brand is Maldon, but there are many on the market. A pinch of flaky sea salt on vegetables, meat, fish, cookies, or even oats(!) can nudge a dish from blah to brilliant . . . especially for little eaters ready to reject anything unfamiliar (or green).

SUGAR: The AAP recommends avoiding added sugars for a baby's first year of life. What is an added sugar? As the name suggests, it's sugar—or maple syrup, corn syrup, molasses, or many other sweeteners (see the box on the opposite page)—that are added to a food during processing. I am not talking about foods with natural sugars, such as plain yogurt, fruit, or some vegetables. Because they are usually found in combination with other nutrients like protein and fiber, most natural sugars won't spike blood sugar as quickly as added sugars. Most foods with natural sugars are well worth feeding your baby.

All this said, I believe it's okay to make the occasional exception to the no-added-sugar rule. If you have made homemade banana bread (such as the low-sugar recipe on page 119), let your baby taste it. If a sauce you're making needs a pinch of sugar to balance out the acid, that's completely okay. Just don't fill your baby's bottle with soda (or juice!), offer him sweetened yogurt, or get him hooked on chocolate just yet.

DAILY FEEDING SCHEDULE AND SUGGESTED PORTION SIZES

It's useful to have a general guide for how much and when to feed your baby. But don't worry if your little one eats more or less than what you see in this chart. Their appetites vary on a weekly—even daily!—basis. As long as your baby is gaining weight normally, follow her lead during feeding.

Since most babies are not able to self-feed before six months of age, serving sizes of fruit, vegetable, and protein purées are included only in tablespoons for babies ages four to six months.

If you're serving mixed meals—say, beef stew with veggies—don't feel the need to measure out every carrot and chunk of beef. In general, just feed your baby a variety of grains, fruits, vegetables, dairy, and protein sources. This chart can help nudge you in the direction of a balanced diet.

one serving

protein	grain	fruit or vegetable	dairy
¼ egg, 2 thin strips of chicken, ½ meatball, 1 ounce of fish, or 2 tablespoons purée. Good protein choices include meat, fish, poultry, eggs, tofu, and beans and lentils.	½ cup cooked oatmeal, rice, quinoa, pasta, or couscous, 2 slices baked oatmeal, or ½ slice toast, cut into sticks	2 pieces, such as 2 slices of soft pear or steamed apple, 2 steamed carrot sticks, ¼ medium avocado, 2 small steamed broccoli florets, or 2 tablespoons purée	½ cup (4 ounces) full-fat yogurt or milk, ¾ ounce full-fat cheese, shredded or cut into thin sticks. Cow's milk is not recommended for infants under 12 months as a main drink, but yogurt or cheese are fine.

	4 TO 6 MONTHS	6 TO 8 MONTHS	8 TO 10 MONTHS	10 TO 12 MONTHS
First thing in the morning	Breastmilk on demand or 6 to 7 ounces of formula	Breastmilk on demand or 6 to 7 ounces of formula	Breastmilk on demand or 6 ounces of formula	Breastmilk on demand or 6 ounces of formula
Breakfast	1 to 2 tablespoons of cereal 1 to 2 tablespoons of fruit or vegetable	2 to 4 tablespoons of cereal or ½ to 1 serving of grain 1 to 2 servings of fruit or vegetable	4 to 6 tablespoons of cereal or 1 to 2 servings of grain 1 to 2 servings of fruit or vegetable	4 to 6 tablespoons of cereal or 1 to 2 servings of grain 2 servings of fruit or vegetable
Midmorning	Breastmilk on demand or 6 to 7 ounces of formula	Breastmilk on demand or 6 to 7 ounces of formula	Breastmilk on demand or 6 ounces of formula	1 serving of dairy and 1 serving of fruit or vegetable
Lunch	1 to 2 tablespoons of cereal 1 to 2 tablespoons of fruit or vegetable OR Breastmilk on demand or 6 to 7 ounces of formula	1 to 2 servings of fruit or vegetable ½ to 1 serving of grain Breastmilk on demand or 6 to 7 ounces of formula	1 to 2 servings of protein 1 to 2 servings of fruit or vegetable 1 serving of grain Breastmilk on demand or 6 ounces of formula	1 to 2 servings of protein 1 to 2 servings of fruit or vegetable 1 serving of grain Breastmilk on demand or 6 ounces of formula
Midafternoon	Breastmilk on demand or 6 to 7 ounces of formula	Breastmilk on demand or 6 to 7 ounces of formula OR 1 serving of dairy	1 to 2 servings of fruit or vegetable 1 serving of grain OR 1 serving of dairy	1 to 2 servings of fruit or vegetable 1 serving of grain OR 1 serving of dairy
Dinner	Breastmilk on demand or 6 to 7 ounces of formula	½ to 1 serving of protein 1 to 2 servings of fruit or vegetable ½ to 1 serving of grain	1 to 2 servings of protein 1 to 2 servings of fruit or vegetable 1 serving of grain	1 to 2 servings of protein 2 servings of fruit or vegetable 1 serving of grain
Before bed	Breastmilk on demand or 6 to 7 ounces of formula	Breastmilk on demand or 6 to 7 ounces of formula	Breastmilk on demand or 6 ounces of formula	Breastmilk on demand or 6 ounces of formula

IMPORTANT NUTRIENTS FOR BABIES

If your baby eats a wide variety of fruits, vegetables, grains, dairy, and meat complemented by breast-milk or formula, chances are he'll be getting all the nutrition he needs to grow and thrive. However, there are a few crucial nutrients that are worth paying special attention to, either because they're especially important to your baby's growth and development, or because the recommended daily amount can be a challenge to reach.

IRON allows blood cells to carry oxygen through the body and is vital for brain development. Insufficient iron intake can lead to impaired cognitive, motor, and behavioral development. Some of these negative effects cannot be reversed. During periods of rapid growth, the need for iron increases.

There are two types of iron in foods: heme iron and non-heme iron. Heme iron is found in animal products like meat, poultry, and seafood, and is easily absorbed by the body. Non-heme iron is found in plants and iron-fortified foods such as some cereals, tofu, beans, lentils, and dark leafy green vegetables like spinach and kale. It is less easily absorbed. However, pairing non-heme iron with vitamin C–rich foods can help with its absorption. These include citrus fruits, berries, sweet potatoes, tomatoes, and broccoli. Once your baby starts solid foods, make sure to include foods that are high in iron. Offer at least two iron-rich foods every day.

ZINC is crucial for proper growth and development, a healthy appetite, and a strong immune system. Human bodies cannot store zinc effectively, so we need a consistent supply through our diets. Once your baby starts solids, make sure to include zinc-rich foods daily in order to avoid deficiency.

Both iron and zinc share common food sources, including meat, fortified breakfast cereals, and some vegetables. This is one of the reasons experts now recommend introducing meat into babies' diets early on. Formula is fortified with iron and zinc, but if your baby is breastfed, it is important to make sure his diet includes solid-food sources of these nutrients by six months of age. You can also talk to your pediatrician about a supplement.

DHA (docosahexaenoic acid) is a type of omega-3 fat that plays a critical role in brain and eye development during the first 24 months of life. Some DHA is found in breastmilk, but the amount is based on the mother's diet; certain formulas are fortified with this important nutrient. The best food sources of DHA are fatty fish and DHA-enriched eggs. Fish and shellfish that are lower in mercury are safer for your baby, so choose salmon, pollock, trout, catfish, canned light tuna, and shrimp. Skip the shark, swordfish, and king mackerel.

recommended daily amounts for babies

Iron (11mg)	Zinc (3mg)	Omega-3 DHA (100–150mg)	Vitamin D (400IU)	Calcium (260mg)	Total fat (30g)
Breakfast cereals, fortified with 100% of the RDV for iron, 1 serving (check the label for serving size) = 18mg	Beef, cooked, 3 ounces = 7mg	Salmon, wild, cooked, 3 ounces = 1,240mg	Salmon, wild, cooked, 3 ounces = 566IU	Cheddar cheese, 1½ ounces = 307mg	Breastmilk, 8 ounces = 11g
Tofu, regular ½ cup = 3mg	Breakfast cereal, fortified with 25% of the RDV for zinc, ¾ cup = 3.8mg	Sardines, canned in oil, drained, 3 ounces = 740mg	Tuna, light, canned in water, drained, 3 ounces = 154IU	Ready-to-eat cereal, calcium-fortified, ½ cup = 50 to 500mg	Full-fat yogurt, 8 ounces = 18g
Lentils, cooked, ½ cup = 3mg	Pork chop, cooked, 3 ounces = 2.9mg	Mackerel, cooked, 3 ounces = 590mg	Orange juice, fortified with vitamin D, 1 cup = 137IU	Tofu, firm, made with calcium sulfate, ½ cup = 253mg	Peanut butter, 1 tablespoon = 8g
Beef, cooked, 3 ounces = 2mg	Chicken, dark meat, cooked, 3 ounces = 2.4mg	Tuna, light, canned in water, drained, 3 ounces = 170mg	Yogurt, fortified with 20% of the RDV for vitamin D, 6 ounces = 80IU	Yogurt, full-fat, plain, 1 cup = 250mg	Avocado, ¼ = 6g
Chicken, cooked, 3 ounces = 1mg	Chickpeas, cooked, ½ cup = 1.3mg	Shrimp, cooked, 3 ounces = 170mg	Sardines, canned in oil, drained, 2 sardines = 46IU	Cottage cheese, full fat, 1 cup = 174mg	Olive oil, 1 teaspoon = 4.5g
Raisins, seedless, ¼ cup = 1mg	Kidney beans, cooked, ½ cup = 0.9mg	Egg, DHA-enriched, 1 large = up to 150mg	Egg, 1 large (vitamin D is found in yolk) 6 ounces = 41IU	Kale, cooked, 1 cup = 94mg	Egg, boiled, 1 large = 4.5g
Egg, 1 large = 1mg	Egg, 1 large = 0.65mg	Cod, cooked, 3 ounces = 100mg	Breakfast cereal, fortified with 10% of the RDV for vitamin D, 1 cup = 40IU	Broccoli, cooked, ½ cup = 31mg	Butter, 1 teaspoon = 4g
Broccoli, cooked, ½ cup = 1mg	Green peas, cooked, ½ cup = 0.5mg	Chicken breast, cooked, 3 ounces = 20mg	Swiss cheese, 1 ounce = 6IU	Whole wheat bread, 1 slice = 30mg	Cheddar cheese, full fat, 1 ounce = 1.5g

Nutrient amounts in specific foods are approximate. Values vary based on origin of the food, cut of meat, and brand.

VITAMIN D helps the body absorb calcium and maintain healthy bones. It is also involved in nerve and muscle function and plays a role in immune system function. Vitamin D has been associated with a lower risk of numerous chronic conditions including type 2 diabetes, high blood pressure, and heart disease. Food sources of this vitamin are sparse. Your baby can also get this "sunshine vitamin" with regular exposure to sunlight, but logistically that can be a challenge. If your baby has limited time in the sunlight or is dark-skinned, make sure to discuss supplementation with your doctor or registered dietitian.

CALCIUM helps build bones and teeth, and promotes muscle contraction, nerve impulse transmission, blood clotting, and hormone secretion. Breastmilk and formula provide much of the calcium your baby needs. Once your baby reaches 12 months, whole cow's milk can be introduced in place of breastmilk or formula. Milk is a rich source of calcium, as are other dairy products like yogurt, cottage cheese, and cheese.

TOTAL FAT is an important part of your baby's diet for satiety, vitamin absorption, and brain development. Almost 50 percent of the calories in your baby's diet should come from fat during the first year of life; neither total fat nor saturated fat should be restricted. To ensure that your baby gets enough, choose full-fat dairy products (like yogurt and cheese) and add olive oil, avocado oil, or butter to foods you prepare. Also, avoid low-fat and nonfat dairy in the first year.

WHAT YOU NEED TO KNOW ABOUT FOOD ALLERGIES

Until recently, parents were advised to introduce the most highly allergenic foods after one or even two years. However, in 2008 the AAP retracted its previous guidelines, saying there was not enough evidence to link a delayed introduction to a decreased risk of food allergy. In fact, research suggests that delaying the introduction of these foods can do the opposite—it can actually lead to an *increased* risk of food allergy!

In 2013 the AAAAI released new guidelines on feeding babies highly allergenic foods. Between ages four and six months, single-ingredient foods—such as rice or oat cereal, yellow and orange vegetables (like sweet potatoes and carrots), fruits (like apples and pears), green vegetables, and meats—which complement breastmilk or formula, should be introduced. After your baby has tried several of these foods, the highly allergenic foods can be introduced one at a time. You can offer your baby the potential allergen alone or together with a food your baby has already eaten and you know they are not allergic to.

Any new food, especially the highly allergenic foods, should be introduced at home, not at a restaurant or daycare center. Start with a very small amount in the morning, which allows you or your baby's caregiver to keep an eye on your baby throughout the day. If your baby hasn't shown any reaction to a newly introduced highly allergenic food, continue feeding your baby that food over the next days and weeks, increasing the amount slowly over time. When you're ready to introduce nuts, skip whole nuts or gobs of nut butter, since they are choking hazards. Instead, stir some nut butter or powder into a purée or spread a thin layer on toast.

The only foods that you should delay feeding your baby until age one are honey (since it might be tainted with botulism) and cow's milk, but for reasons unrelated to food allergies. Both cheese and yogurt can be introduced earlier, when your baby is ready, and in the same manner as the other highly allergenic foods. It's also okay to use some milk in baking or cooking for your baby.

these foods are considered the most highly allergenic:

- Peanuts
- Tree nuts
- Soy
- Fish
- Shellfish
- Eggs
- Dairy
- Wheat

The introduction of any food, including those that are highly allergenic, should be a positive experience for your baby. It's your decision in which order to introduce these foods. If your baby has eczema or signs of a food allergy, or if you have another child with a peanut allergy, talk to your pediatrician about how to proceed.

Signs of Mild Allergic Reaction

If you notice any of these symptoms, stop serving the food and speak with your pediatrician.

- ▶ Hives
- ▶ Eczema
- ▶ Redness of the skin around the eyes
- ▶ Stomach pain
- ▶ Sneezing
- ▶ A dry cough
- ▶ Nausea or vomiting
- ▶ Diarrhea
- ▶ Itchy mouth

Signs of Severe Allergic Reaction

If your baby exhibits a severe symptom call 911 or get to the nearest emergency room right away.

- ▶ Swelling of lips, tongue, or throat
- ▶ Difficulty swallowing
- ▶ Shortness of breath
- ▶ Turning blue
- ▶ Loss of consciousness
- ▶ Chest pain
- ▶ A weak pulse

9 ways to raise a happy eater right from the start

1. **Follow your baby's cues if you're spoon-feeding.** If she closes her mouth, turns away, or starts fussing, mealtime is over. The high chair should be a pressure-free zone.

2. **Let your baby play with her food.** Touching, smelling, exploring, and, yes, tasting foods can help your child become familiar with and more accepting of new flavors.

3. **Whenever possible, eat the same foods at the same time.** Let your child see how you eat and that, since you're a family, you eat the same foods together.

4. **Serve a fruit or vegetable at every meal and snack.** It won't happen every time, but make produce a normal, expected part of your child's daily meals and snacks.

5. **Put on a variety show.** Studies have shown that the more foods babies try before age one, the more foods they're likely to enjoy as an older kid. Vary texture as well.

6. **Remember your job, and let your child do hers.** Your responsibility is to provide a variety of healthy, appealing foods. It's your baby's job to decide what and how much to eat.

7. **Strike a healthy balance.** Don't cater only to your baby's current preferences at mealtime, but make sure there's something in the mix that he enjoys.

8. **Be tenacious.** When a child doesn't like a food, that often just means she isn't familiar with it. Continue offering the food, switching up the cooking method, temperature of the food, and even its texture (finely chopped vs. puréed, for example) from time to time.

9. **Keep calm.** Stress and anxiety at the table are not conducive to adventurous eating. Make mealtime about talking and connecting, not policing the number of bites your baby eats.

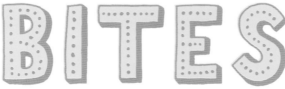

CHAPTER TWO
SIMPLE BITES
····(6-8 months)····

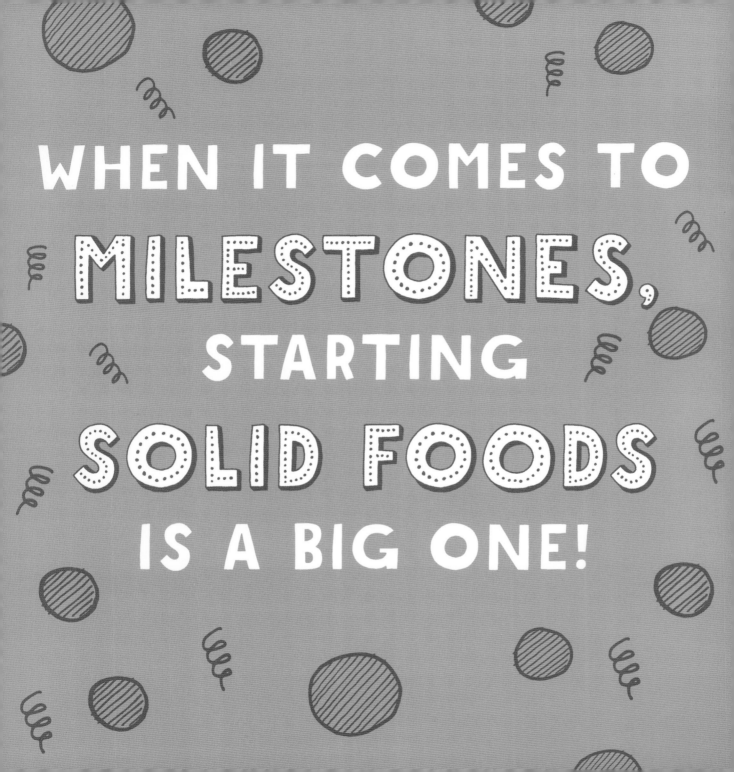

WHEN IT COMES TO **MILESTONES,** STARTING **SOLID FOODS** IS A BIG ONE!

Enjoy introducing new foods to your little one, and remember that at this stage, it's more about exploration, taste training, and getting the mechanics of eating down than it is about making sure your baby eats a certain amount or gets all her vegetable servings in. At this point, your baby will still be getting the majority of her nutrition from breastmilk or formula.

Most of the recipes in this chapter are for purées, but many can also be served as finger foods; these are marked with the 🖐 icon. Remember, it's okay to mix it up and serve both a purée and a finger food at the same meal. Just don't put two textures on the same spoon. Figuring out how to handle a purée and a solid food in the same bite can be a challenge for younger babies.

Most of the recipes in this chapter come with Flavor Kick suggestions, ideas for adding extra flavor to a basic purée. I've also included Purée Playdate suggestions, recommendations for which purées mix well together.

The serving sizes in this chapter are quite small, usually 2 tablespoons. Your baby might eat less or more in one sitting, and that's perfectly fine. Make sure the high chair is a pressure-free zone. The more enjoyable eating is for your baby, the more likely she'll be to want to eat a variety of foods.

A few safety basics:

▶ Food that comes out of a multi-cooker is HOT. Make sure whatever you serve your baby is just barely warm, at room temperature, or cold.

▶ Place just a little purée in a bowl or a few finger foods on your baby's tray to start. Anything she doesn't eat should be discarded, so it's better to begin with less and add more if your baby is especially hungry.

▶ If a purée is too thick for your baby to handle, you can thin it out with a little breastmilk, formula, or water. If it's too thin, stir in a little baby cereal or a thicker purée.

Now dish it up, sit back, and get ready for your baby's eating adventure to begin!

asparagus
page 45

cauliflower
page 56

beet
page 50

apple
page 44

butternut squash
page 53

PURÉES

APPLES ❄ ⓷⓪

4 Gala apples (2 pounds), peeled, cored, and sliced

½ cup water

Pear Variation: *Follow the same procedure using 6 ripe Bartlett pears (peeled, halved, and cored) and ¼ cup water. Makes about 2 cups.*

Flavor Kick: *To either the apples or pears, stir in a pinch of ground cinnamon or cardamom after puréeing. These purées are also delicious with a little peanut butter or almond butter stirred in after cooking and puréeing. Mix well to be sure no clumps remain.*

Purée Playdates: *Potato, sweet potato, beef, broccoli, spinach, lamb, chicken, turkey, beans*

You may have heard that if you start solids with fruit, babies are less likely to enjoy vegetables. There's no evidence that this is the case; babies already naturally prefer sweet flavors—after all, breastmilk is a little sweet. So don't be afraid to introduce fruit early on. This wholesome purée was the first solid food I offered my daughter, and I promise that she likes salad.

1 Place the apple slices in the cooker. Pour in the water. Lock the lid and set to cook on high pressure for 3 minutes. When cooking is complete, press "Cancel" and carefully quick-release the pressure.

2 Remove the lid and let the apples cool slightly. Using an immersion blender, blend until smooth.

Makes about 2½ cups

SLOW COOK IT: Place the apples in a slow cooker with 1 cup water, cover, and cook on Low for 4 to 6 hours, or until very tender.

Apples Nutrition per serving (2 tablespoons): 22 calories; 0g protein; 0g fat (0g sat. fat); 6g carbohydrates; 1g fiber; 5g sugars; 0mg sodium; 2mg calcium; 0mg iron; 41mg potassium; 2mg vitamin C; 17IU vitamin A

Pears Nutrition per serving (2 tablespoons): 38 calories; 0g protein; 0g fat (0g sat. fat); 10g carbohydrates; 2g fiber; 7g sugars; 1mg sodium; 6mg calcium; 0.1mg iron; 77mg potassium; 3mg vitamin C; 17IU vitamin A

ASPARAGUS

Asparagus can be one of the trickier veggies for kids to love, so start your baby on it early and remember it can take several exposures for him to enjoy it. And while there's no guarantee that a baby who likes asparagus will turn into a kid who likes asparagus, you'll have much better odds.

¾ cup water

2 bunches asparagus (about 2 pounds total), woody ends snapped off

1 Pour the water into the multi-cooker. Add the asparagus. Lock the lid and set to cook on high pressure for 2 to 3 minutes (use 3 minutes for thicker spears). When cooking is complete, press "Cancel" and carefully quick-release the pressure.

2 Remove the lid and let the asparagus cool slightly. Using an immersion blender, blend until smooth.

Makes about 2½ cups

Nutrition per serving (2 tablespoons): 9 calories; 1g protein; 0g fat (0g sat. fat); 2g carbohydrates; 1g fiber; 1g sugars; 1mg sodium; 11mg calcium; 1mg iron; 92mg potassium; 3mg vitamin C; 343IU vitamin A

Flavor Kick: *A little grated Parmesan cheese can help tame asparagus's bitterness. Stir it in before blending or sprinkle it on top if serving asparagus spears as a finger food.*

Purée Playdates: *Potato, sweet potato, zucchini, beef, chicken, butternut squash, lamb, beans*

Make It a Finger Food: *Cut asparagus spears into 2- to 3-inch pieces. It can be hard for babies to gum through the outer skin of the asparagus, so think of asparagus spear–eating more as play and exploration than nourishment. And did you know that according to etiquette experts, asparagus should be eaten with your fingers? In this case, your baby is already being oh-so-polite.*

BEANS AND SPLIT PEAS

7 cups water

2 cups dried beans or split peas (about 1 pound), rinsed

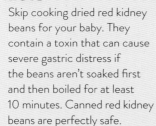

food safety note

Skip cooking dried red kidney beans for your baby. They contain a toxin that can cause severe gastric distress if the beans aren't soaked first and then boiled for at least 10 minutes. Canned red kidney beans are perfectly safe.

Age It Up: *Add 2 teaspoons kosher salt before pressure cooking.*

Beans are great for your baby, and multi-cookers are great for beans. That's what I call a win-win! The best part about cooking beans in your multi-cooker is that they don't have to be soaked first, so it's truly possible to cook dried beans in under an hour.

Just to note, I am not anti-canned beans. They are an inexpensive, ultra-convenient, very healthy food. But beans cooked from dried taste about 1,000% better. You're also left with the flavorful cooking liquid, which can serve as a soup base or be used to help loosen up a purée. Plus, when you cook your own beans, you can omit salt if you like. There are no-salt-added canned beans on the market, but they can be difficult to find. If you do opt for canned beans and can only find regular or low-sodium, studies show that rinsing them reduces the sodium by up to 40 percent.

1 Add the water and the beans or split peas to the multi-cooker. Lock the lid and set to cook on high pressure for the time indicated in the chart on the next page. When cooking is complete, press "Cancel" and, if you have time, let the pressure release naturally for best texture. If not, it's okay to quick-release the pressure.

2 Remove the lid and let the beans cool slightly. If serving as a finger food, smash each bean lightly with your fingers. If puréeing, drain the beans, reserving the cooking liquid. Return the beans to the pot along with ½ cup of the reserved cooking liquid. Using an immersion blender, blend until smooth, adding more cooking liquid as needed.

Makes about 6 cups

SLOW COOK IT: Soak the beans in water to cover overnight. Drain and transfer to a slow cooker with 7 cups water. Cover and cook on High for 5 to 6 hours, or until tender.

Bean	Time
Black beans	20 to 30 minutes
Cannellini beans	35 to 40 minutes
Chickpeas	35 to 40 minutes
Navy beans	25 to 30 minutes
Pinto beans	25 to 35 minutes
Split peas	15 to 20 minutes

Storage Tip: Refrigerate or freeze beans covered in their cooking water.

BEETS ❄

½ cup water

4 medium beets (about ¾ pound), scrubbed and trimmed

Flavor Kick: *Stir finely chopped fresh dill and/or plain Greek yogurt into the finished purée.*

Purée Playdates: *Potato, sweet potato, beef, chicken, lamb, turkey, salmon, lentils, cauliflower*

Cooking beets in a multi-cooker means you don't need to peel them first. If having pink hands for a few hours bothers you, wear plastic gloves when peeling the beets after cooking. And PSA: Don't be surprised to see red in your baby's diaper after she eats beets. It's completely harmless.

• •

1 Pour the water into the multi-cooker. Place the wire rack that came with the multi-cooker into the pot. Place the beets on the rack. Lock the lid and set to cook on high pressure for 15 to 20 minutes, depending on the size of the beets. When cooking is complete, press "Cancel" and carefully quick-release the pressure.

2 Transfer the beets to a plate to cool, reserving the water in the cooker. When cool enough to handle, peel the beets and discard the skins.

3 Chop the beets and return them to the liquid in the cooker. Using an immersion blender, blend until smooth.

Makes about 1½ cups

• •

SLOW COOK IT: Peel and chop 1 pound beets. Add to a slow cooker with ¼ cup water. Cover and cook on Low for 6 hours or until very tender. Blend until smooth.

• •

Nutrition per serving (2 tablespoons): 12 calories; 0g protein; 0g fat (0g sat. fat); 3g carbohydrates; 1g fiber; 2g sugars; 22mg sodium; 5mg calcium; 0.2mg iron; 92mg potassium; 1mg vitamin C; 9IU vitamin A

BELL PEPPERS ❄ ㉚

Look for red, orange, or yellow bells (or a combo) for this recipe. Green bell peppers are more bitter and less delicious.

• •

1 Pour the water into the multi-cooker. Add the peppers. Lock the lid and set to cook on high pressure for 2 minutes. When cooking is complete, press "Cancel" and carefully quick-release the pressure.

2 Transfer the peppers to a bowl, reserving the water in the cooker. Cover the bowl with plastic wrap and let the peppers steam for 10 minutes.

3 When the peppers are cool enough to handle, peel them and discard the skins. Return the peppers to the liquid in the pot. Using an immersion blender, blend until smooth.

Makes about 3 cups

• •

Nutrition per serving (2 tablespoons): 6 calories; 0g protein; 0g fat (0g sat. fat); 1g carbohydrates; 0g fiber; 1g sugars; 1mg sodium; 2mg calcium; 0.1mg iron; 42mg potassium; 25mg vitamin C; 621IU vitamin A

½ cup water

4 bell peppers, halved and seeds removed

Flavor Kick: *Mix a teaspoon or two of DIY Walnut Butter (page 134) into the finished purée, making sure no clumps remain.*

Purée Playdates: *Broccoli, cauliflower, sweet potato, potato, carrot, eggplant*

BRUSSELS ❄ 🕧 SPROUTS

¾ cup water

1 pound Brussels sprouts, trimmed

Flavor Kick: *It's a little pricey, but if you happen to have walnut oil on hand, drizzle a bit into the finished purée.*

Purée Playdates: *Beans, salmon, beef, chicken, turkey, sweet potato, potato, lamb*

Help your baby get into the Brussels sprout habit. They're packed with antioxidants, anti-inflammatory compounds, and fiber. Go easy in the early days, though, since these baby cabbages might give your baby gas.

1 Pour the water into the multi-cooker. Add the sprouts. Lock the lid and set to cook on high pressure for 4 minutes. When cooking is complete, press "Cancel" and carefully quick-release the pressure.

2 Remove the lid and let the sprouts cool slightly. Using an immersion blender, blend until smooth.

Makes about 2 cups

Nutrition per serving (2 tablespoons): 12 calories; 1g protein; 0g fat (0g sat. fat); 3g carbohydrates; 1g fiber; 1g sugars; 7mg sodium; 12mg calcium; 0.4mg iron; 110mg potassium; 24mg vitamin C; 214IU vitamin A

BUTTERNUT ❄ SQUASH

You can also start with a package of store-bought peeled and chopped butternut squash. Use a metal steamer basket, and reduce the cooking time to 5 minutes.

1 medium butternut squash
(2½ to 3 pounds)

1½ cups water

. . . .

1 Wash and dry the squash. Cut the squash in half crosswise where the neck meets the bulb. Cut the neck in half lengthwise. Cut the bulb in half lengthwise and remove the seeds.

2 Pour the water into the multi-cooker. Place the metal rack that came with the multi-cooker in the pot. Place the squash pieces on the rack, cut-side up. Lock the lid and set to cook on high pressure for 12 to 15 minutes, depending on the size of the squash. When cooking is complete, press "Cancel" and carefully quick-release the pressure.

3 Remove the lid and let the squash cool slightly. Using a spoon, scoop the squash flesh into a large bowl and discard the skin. Using a fork, mash the flesh until smooth or, for a perfectly smooth purée, blend with an immersion blender or transfer the squash to a food processor and purée.

Makes about 2½ cups

. . . .

SLOW COOK IT: Place 2 pounds chopped peeled butternut squash and ½ cup water in a slow cooker. Cover and cook on Low for 5 to 6 hours, or until tender. Blend until smooth.

. . . .

Acorn Squash Variation: *Halve and seed an acorn squash. Follow the same method, cooking the squash for 15 minutes. If the squash is still a little firm after cooking, place the multi-cooker lid on the pot (don't lock it), and let the squash steam for 5 to 10 minutes more before puréeing.*

Flavor Kick: *Stir a few pinches of smoked paprika or finely chopped fresh sage into the finished purée.*

Purée Playdates: *Zucchini, bell pepper, cauliflower, broccoli, pea, lentils, beef, chicken, lamb, beans*

Nutrition per serving (2 tablespoons): 20 calories; 1g protein; 0g fat (0g sat. fat); 6g carbohydrates; 1g fiber; 1g sugars; 3mg sodium; 27mg calcium; 0.4mg iron; 192mg potassium; 11mg vitamin C; 5,786IU vitamin A

CARROTS

¾ cup water

1 pound carrots, peeled and cut into 2 x ½-inch sticks

Flavor Kick: *Stir ½ teaspoon curry powder, ground cumin, or ground cinnamon into the finished purée.*

Purée Playdates: *Chicken, beef, lamb, beans, lentils, zucchini, spinach, kale*

They may not give your baby X-ray vision, but carrots are packed with beta-carotene, an antioxidant that supports eye health.

1 Pour the water into the multi-cooker. Add the carrots. Lock the lid and set to cook on high pressure for 6 minutes. When cooking is complete, press "Cancel" and carefully quick-release the pressure.

2 Remove the lid and let the carrots cool slightly. Using an immersion blender, blend until smooth.

Makes about 2½ cups

SLOW COOK IT: Peel and chop 2 pounds carrots. Add to a slow cooker with ½ cup water. Cover and cook on Low for 6 hours or until tender, adding more water after 3 hours if the carrots seem dry. Blend until smooth.

Nutrition per serving (2 tablespoons purée): 19 calories; 0g protein; 0g fat (0g sat. fat); 4g carbohydrates; 1g fiber; 2g sugars; 32mg sodium; 15mg calcium; 0.1mg iron; 145mg potassium; 3mg vitamin C; 7,578IU vitamin A

Make It a Finger Food

Cook the carrots for 5 minutes. Let cool and serve; 2 or 3 sticks is a good serving size to start.

CAULIFLOWER ⊛ ❄ ⊗
(OR BROCCOLI!)

¾ cup water

1 large head cauliflower, broken into medium florets, or 1 head broccoli, chopped into medium florets with 1-inch stems (about 8 cups)

Make It a Finger Food: *Cut the cauliflower or broccoli into small florets with 1- to 2-inch "handles" for grasping. Place them in a steamer basket in the multi-cooker instead of directly in the water.*

Flavor Kick: *Stir a bit of olive oil and/or grated Parmesan cheese into the finished purée. Yum!*

Purée Playdates: *Zucchini, chicken, beef, carrot, butternut squash, sweet potato, potato, bell pepper*

If pressed to name my favorite vegetables, I would say broccoli and cauliflower, doubtless because my parents fed me copious amounts of them when I was a baby. (Or so I like to imagine.)

1   Pour the water into the multi-cooker. Add the cauliflower or broccoli. Lock the lid and set to cook on high pressure for 1 minute. When cooking is complete, press "Cancel" and carefully quick-release the pressure.

2   Remove the lid and let the cauliflower or broccoli cool slightly. Using an immersion blender, blend until smooth.

Makes about 4 cups cauliflower purée or 3 cups broccoli purée

SLOW COOK IT: Place the cauliflower or broccoli (or a mix!) and ½ cup water in a slow cooker. Cover and cook on Low for 2 to 3 hours, or until tender.

Cauliflower Nutrition per serving (2 tablespoons purée): 4 calories; 0g protein; 0g fat (0g sat. fat); 1g carbohydrates; 0g fiber; 0g sugars; 6mg sodium; 4mg calcium; 0.1mg iron; 54mg potassium; 9mg vitamin C; 0IU vitamin A

Broccoli Nutrition per serving (2 tablespoons purée): 7 calories; 1g protein; 0g fat (0g sat. fat); 1g carbohydrates; 0g fiber; 0g sugars; 7mg sodium; 12mg calcium; 0.2mg iron; 77mg potassium; 22mg vitamin C; 710IU vitamin A

CHICKEN ✋ ❄ ㉚

Tired of the dry, stringy chicken you get when you bake boneless breasts? Me too. A multi-cooker is the answer. You'll end up with perfectly tender and moist chicken ideal for a purée or finger food.

• •

1 Spray the walls of the cooker with cooking spray.

2 Pour the water into the multi-cooker. Add the chicken. Lock the lid and set to cook on high pressure for 8 to 10 minutes, depending on the thickness of the chicken breasts. When cooking is complete, press "Cancel" and carefully quick-release the pressure.

3 Remove the lid and let the chicken cool slightly. Using an immersion blender, blend until smooth.

Makes 3½ cups

• •

Nutrition per serving (2 tablespoons purée): 26 calories; 5g protein; 1g fat (0g sat. fat); 0g carbohydrates; 0g fiber; 0g sugars; 42mg sodium; 1mg calcium; 0.1mg iron; 81mg potassium; 0mg vitamin C; 9IU vitamin A

Nonstick cooking spray

1 cup water or low-sodium chicken broth

2 boneless, skinless breasts (1 to 1½ pounds total)

Make It a Finger Food: *Cook the chicken as directed, then transfer it to a plate to cool. When it's cool enough to handle, shred the chicken with your fingers or chop it into small pieces. Makes 4 cups shredded or chopped.*

Flavor Kick: *Add a couple of cloves of garlic to the multi-cooker with the chicken before cooking. Purée as directed.*

Purée Playdates: *Apple, pear, potato, sweet potato, zucchini, cauliflower, broccoli, pea, butternut squash, peach*

CUCUMBER

Cooking cucumber may seem counterintuitive, but it makes a delicious, fresh-tasting purée. This one blends up best in a standard blender.

- -

1 Pour the water into the multi-cooker. Add the cucumber. Lock the lid and set to cook on high pressure for 5 minutes. When cooking is complete, press "Cancel" and carefully quick-release the pressure.

2 Remove the lid and let the cucumber cool slightly. Transfer the cucumber and its cooking liquid to a blender and blend until smooth (take care when blending hot foods; see below.)

Makes about 1½ cups

- -

Nutrition per serving (2 tablespoons): 4 calories; 0g protein; 0g fat (0g sat. fat); 1g carbohydrates; 0g fiber; 0g sugars; 1mg sodium; 4mg calcium; 0.1mg iron; 37mg potassium; 1mg vitamin C; 26IU vitamin A

½ cup water

1 English cucumber, trimmed and cut into 1-inch rounds

Flavor Kick: *Add some fresh mint or basil before blending or stir some sesame oil into the finished purée.*

Purée Playdates: *Salmon, chicken, spinach, carrot*

take care!

Be mindful when blending hot liquids, since pressure can build and cause whatever you're blending to spew out, leading to a dangerous mess. To be safe, remove the plastic insert from the blender top and loosely cover the opening with a folded-over dish towel while blending.

HARD-BOILED EGGS

1 cup water

Large eggs

an egg-cellent option

Eggs are often called "the perfect food," and it's easy to see why. Each one contains 6g of protein and 5g of healthy fats. They're also a good source of choline, an essential nutrient for your baby's brain development. It's perfectly fine to offer babies both egg whites (protein!) and egg yolks (healthy fats!). The yolks also contain omega-3s, riboflavin, vitamin D, vitamin B_{12} and selenium. As with every food you serve your baby, keep an eye out for allergic reactions (see page 35). Omelets and scrambled eggs are also easy and nutritious foods for baby. Cook them on the stovetop, chop into small pieces, and serve as a finger food.

This recipe makes as few or as many eggs as you'd like to cook—you can literally fit dozens in the multi-cooker!

1 Pour the water into the multi-cooker. Place the metal rack that came with the multi-cooker in the pot. Pile the eggs on top of the rack. Lock the lid and set to cook on high pressure for 8 minutes.

2 Meanwhile, fill a bowl large enough to fit all the eggs with plenty of room to spare with cold water. Add a few ice cubes.

3 When cooking is complete, press "Cancel" and carefully quick-release the pressure.

4 Transfer the eggs to the ice water and let cool for 10 minutes. Peel and serve, or store unpeeled eggs in the refrigerator for up to 5 days.

Nutrition per serving (½ egg): 39 calories; 3g protein; 3g fat (1g sat. fat); 0g carbohydrates; 0g fiber; 0g sugars; 31mg sodium; 13mg calcium; 0.3mg iron; 32mg potassium; 0mg vitamin C; 130IU vitamin A

3 ways with eggs for babies

1. Cut into wedges or chop into small pieces and serve as a finger food.

2. Chop into small pieces and place in a bowl. Add a spoonful of plain full-fat Greek yogurt and a pinch of ground turmeric. Stir to combine. Serve as a (messy!) finger food or spread on toast sticks.

3. Combine finely chopped egg with finely chopped avocado. Spritz with lemon juice. Stir and serve as a dip for crackers or steamed vegetables.

EGGPLANT ❄ ㉚

½ cup water

1 medium eggplant (about 1½ pounds), trimmed and cut into 8 to 10 pieces

Flavor Kick: *Stir a little tahini into the finished purée, making sure no clumps remain.*

Purée Playdates: *Zucchini, potato, cauliflower, salmon, chicken, lamb, beans, lentils, butternut squash*

Don't be surprised when the eggplant turns grayish after puréeing. It may not be pretty, but it *is* tasty, especially when mixed with tahini (sesame seed paste) or one of the Purée Playdate suggestions I've listed.

1 Pour the water into the multi-cooker. Add a steamer basket and the eggplant. Lock the lid and set to cook on high pressure for 3 minutes. When cooking is complete, press "Cancel" and carefully quick-release the pressure.

2 Remove the lid and let the eggplant cool slightly. Using a slotted spoon, transfer the eggplant to a standard blender and blend until smooth (take care when blending hot foods; see page 59).

Makes 2 cups

SLOW COOK IT: Chop 2 medium eggplants and place in a slow cooker with ¼ cup water. Cover and cook on Low for 3 to 4 hours, until the eggplant is very tender. Blend until smooth.

Nutrition per serving (2 tablespoons): 11 calories; 0g protein; 0g fat (0g sat. fat); 3g carbohydrates; 1g fiber; 2g sugars; 1mg sodium; 4mg calcium; 0.1mg iron; 97mg potassium; 1mg vitamin C; 10IU vitamin A

GREEN BEANS

Thanks to their long, skinny shape, green beans are a natural finger food. But they also blend up beautifully in a standard blender.

½ cup water

1 pound green beans, trimmed

1 Pour the water into the multi-cooker. Add the green beans. Lock the lid and set to cook on high pressure for 3 minutes. When cooking is complete, press "Cancel" and carefully quick-release the pressure.

2 Remove the lid and let the green beans cool slightly. Transfer to a standard blender with the cooking liquid and blend until smooth (take care when blending hot foods; see page 59).

Makes 2 cups

SLOW COOK IT: Place 1½ pounds trimmed green beans and 1 cup water in a slow cooker. Cover and cook on High for 2 to 3 hours, or until tender. Blend until smooth.

Make It a Finger Food: *Reduce the cooking time to 2 minutes; drain off the liquid after cooking.*

Flavor Kick: *Stir a spoonful of almond butter into the finished purée, making sure no clumps remain.*

Purée Playdates: *Potato, sweet potato, cauliflower, beef, chicken, lentils, beans, turkey, lamb, carrot, butternut squash*

Nutrition per serving (2 tablespoons purée): 9 calories; 1g protein; 0g fat (0g sat. fat); 2g carbohydrates; 1g fiber; 1g sugars; 2mg sodium; 11mg calcium; 0.3mg iron; 60mg potassium; 3mg vitamin C; 196IU vitamin A

the bitter and the sweet

If your baby doesn't like a bitter vegetable purée like kale or broccoli, should you mix it with a sweeter fruit purée? That strategy seems to make perfect sense, and in fact it's one I used to advocate. After all, we want our babies to eat veggies! But actually, what we really should want is for our babies to learn to *like* veggies. And they can't learn that lesson if all the vegetables they eat taste like fruit. Instead, try mixing the offending vegetable purée with a more neutral flavor like potato or chicken. The bitterness will be diluted, but still present in a way that hopefully your little one will learn to appreciate.

KALE ❄ ③

Kale isn't just for trendy salads; it's also an ultra-nutritious food for babies and an easy way to introduce your little one to bitter flavors (see the opposite page). There's no need to thoroughly dry the kale after washing it. This is one of those recipes where it's best to use a standard blender for a smoother and less stringy purée. You can use this same method for collard greens and Swiss chard.

¾ cup water

1 small bunch curly kale (about 8 ounces), stemmed, or about 14 cups chopped kale

Flavor Kick: *Drizzle a bit of olive oil into the finished purée and spritz with lemon juice.*

Purée Playdates: *Potato, chicken, cauliflower, pea, carrot, salmon, butternut squash*

• •

1 Pour the water into the multi-cooker. Add the kale. Lock the lid and set to cook on high pressure for 3 minutes. When cooking is complete, press "Cancel" and carefully quick-release the pressure.

2 Remove the lid and let the kale cool slightly. Transfer the kale and its cooking liquid to a standard blender and blend until smooth (take care when blending hot foods; see page 59).

Makes about 1¼ cups

• •

Nutrition per serving (2 tablespoons): 11 calories; 1g protein; 0g fat (0g sat. fat); 2g carbohydrates; 1g fiber; 1g sugars; 9mg sodium; 35mg calcium; 0.3mg iron; 112mg potassium; 27mg vitamin C; 2,266IU vitamin A

MEAT ✋ ❄️ ⏱️

1 pound boneless beef, pork, or lamb stew meat, trimmed of fat and cut into 1-inch pieces

½ to ¾ cup water

Flavor Kick: *Stir a little tomato paste into the finished purée for a savory boost.*

Purée Playdates: *Apple, potato, sweet potato, broccoli, cauliflower, butternut squash, pea, spinach, kale, pear*

A plain, unseasoned meat purée may not seem like a typical baby food—but remember that breastfed babies over the age of six months need good sources of iron, zinc, and protein in their diets. Beef, pork, and lamb fit the bill, whether you serve them as a finger food or purée. Adding a Flavor Kick or a Purée Playdate can help alleviate any parental squeamishness. Remove and discard any large chunks of fat before cooking.

1 Place the meat and ½ cup water in the multi-cooker. Lock the lid and set to cook on high pressure for 30 minutes. When cooking is complete, press "Cancel" and let the pressure release naturally, 5 to 10 minutes. Carefully quick-release any remaining pressure.

2 Use a slotted spoon to transfer the meat to a large bowl or cutting board. Discard the liquid in the pot. If serving as a finger food, shred the meat with your fingers or two forks. If serving as a puree, transfer the meat back to the pot, add ¼ cup fresh water, and purée with an immersion blender until smooth.

Makes 1½ cups purée or 2 cups shredded

Beef Nutrition per serving (2 tablespoons purée): 48 calories; 8g protein; 2g fat (1g sat. fat); 0g carbohydrates; 0g fiber; 0g sugars; 31mg sodium; 5mg calcium; 0.8mg iron; 139mg potassium; 0mg vitamin C; 2IU vitamin A

Lamb Nutrition per serving (2 tablespoons purée): 51 calories; 8g protein; 2g fat (1g sat. fat); 0g carbohydrates; 0g fiber; 0g sugars; 25mg sodium; 3mg calcium; 0.7mg iron; 108mg potassium; 0mg vitamin C; 0IU vitamin A

Pork Nutrition per serving (2 tablespoons purée): 46 calories; 8g protein; 1g fat (1g sat. fat); 0g carbohydrates; 0g fiber; 0g sugars; 25mg sodium; 3mg calcium; 0.3mg iron; 142mg potassium; 0mg vitamin C; 3IU vitamin A

SLOW COOK IT: Place the meat and water in a slow cooker. Cover and cook on Low for 7 to 8 hours, until the meat is completely tender and there's no pink remaining.

picky, picky

If your baby turns up her nose at cauliflower or spits Brussels sprouts out with what looks like disgust, it may be tempting to proclaim, "Welp, she doesn't like it!" and throw the remainder of the offending food in the trash.

The truth is, for most babies the bitter flavors of many veggies (or the earthy taste of lamb, for example) may not be instant winners. It takes time and multiple exposures for your baby to become familiar with a food and then hopefully accept it. She won't like everything, but if you keep serving her foods she's less certain of, she'll end up enjoying many of them.

If you're offering purées, one strategy I like for encouraging more variety is mixing a stronger-flavored purée that your baby doesn't love yet—such as asparagus, broccoli, or spinach—with a milder purée like potato or chicken. This will help temper some of the veggie's bitter flavors. I'm less of a fan of mixing a savory purée with a sweet one. This is a trick employed by many pouched purées. The pouch contains, say, kale, but masks the flavor with sweet butternut squash and apple, for example. Our job as parents isn't to make sure our babies eat kale, but to help them *learn to like* kale. If we're always covering up the vegetable's flavor, babies will never have the chance to learn to enjoy it.

And not to be the bearer of bad news, but know that just because your baby relishes carrots now doesn't mean she'll continue to love them when she's two or three. Many children go through a choosy phase from about ages two to five. The more flavors she learns to like now, though, the more she's likely to enjoy when she's older . . . even if she takes a little break during her toddler years.

For now, when your baby is making hilarious faces trying new foods, try not to prejudge her reaction. She may screw up her face in what looks like repulsion, then take a second bite, and then a third. Just be sure to take lots of photos.

> **OUR JOB AS PARENTS ISN'T TO MAKE SURE OUR BABIES EAT KALE, BUT TO HELP THEM LEARN TO LIKE KALE.**

PEACHES

½ cup water

4 ripe peaches, halved and pitted

Flavor Kick: *Stir a little almond butter into the finished purée, making sure no clumps remain.*

Purée Playdates: *Apple, potato, pear, beef, chicken, turkey, beans*

Make It a Finger Food: *After cooking, peel the peaches and chop them into chickpea-size pieces. (Nectarines will likely be too soft to chop, so save them for puréeing.)*

A multi-cooker makes preparing peach purée a snap. If you were cooking this sweet sauce on the stovetop, you'd need to first blanch the peaches in boiling water, peel them, and *then* steam them. No thanks!

Peaches are one of a few fruits (also plums and cherries) that I only serve when they're in season. A hard, dry peach is just wrong. So make this recipe when peaches are ripe and juicy; that's July, August, and a little bit of September where I live. Prep extra to freeze; you and your baby will be thankful for a spoonful of fragrant peaches come winter.

You can cook nectarines using this same method, but I've found that the skins don't slip off as easily. No worries—just blend nectarines with their skins on. They are thinner than peach skins and disappear into the purée.

. . . .

1 Pour the water into the multi-cooker. Add the peaches, skin-side down. Lock the lid and set to cook on high pressure for 4 minutes. When cooking is complete, press "Cancel" and carefully quick-release the pressure.

2 Using a slotted spoon, transfer the peaches to a plate to cool, reserving the liquid in the cooker. When the peaches are cool enough to handle, peel them and discard the skins.

(continues)

3 Return the peaches to the liquid in the cooker. Using an immersion blender, blend until smooth.

Makes about 2 cups

. . . .

SLOW COOK IT: Bring a large pot of water to a boil. Cut a small "x" in the underside of 6 to 8 peaches. Add the peaches to the boiling water and blanch for 1 minute. Using a slotted spoon, transfer the peaches to a bowl and let cool. Peel the peaches, discarding the skins, then halve and pit them. Transfer the peach halves to a slow cooker and add ½ cup water. Cover and cook on Low for 3 to 4 hours, stirring once during the cooking time. Blend until smooth.

. . . .

Nutrition per serving (2 tablespoons purée): 15 calories; 0g protein; 0g fat (0g sat. fat); 4g carbohydrates; 1g fiber; 3g sugars; 0mg sodium; 2mg calcium; 0.1mg iron; 71mg potassium; 2mg vitamin C; 122IU vitamin A

PLUMS ❄ ⓷⓪

Plum purée is more tart than you might think, since you blend the skins with the flesh. This purée is on the thin side. Mix it with Greek yogurt for a delicious breakfast or snack. A little plum purée can also help relieve constipation.

½ cup water

8 plums (about 1½ pounds), halved and pitted

Flavor Kick: *Stir a few pinches of ground cardamom into the finished purée.*

Purée Playdates: *Apple, peach, potato, beef, chicken, turkey, lamb, lentils, beans*

1 Pour the water into the multi-cooker. Place the plums in the pot, skin-side down. Lock the lid and set to cook on high pressure for 2 minutes. When cooking is complete, press "Cancel" and carefully quick-release the pressure.

2 Remove the lid and let the plums cool slightly. Using an immersion blender, blend until smooth, skins and all.

Makes about 3 cups

> **SLOW COOK IT:** Halve and pit 3 pounds of plums. Transfer the plum halves to a slow cooker and add ½ cup water. Cover and cook on Low for 1 to 2 hours, stirring once during the cooking time. Blend until smooth.

Nutrition per serving (2 tablespoons): 10 calories; 0g protein; 0g fat (0g sat. fat); 3g carbohydrates; 0g fiber; 2g sugars; 0mg sodium; 1mg calcium; 0mg iron; 35mg potassium; 2mg vitamin C; 76U vitamin A

POTATOES 🖐 ❄️
OR SWEET POTATOES

2 large russet potatoes
or sweet potatoes (about
1½ pounds total)

1 cup water

Flavor Kick: *Stir 1 tablespoon unsalted butter or olive oil into the finished purée for a boost of both flavor and healthy fats.*

Purée Playdates: *Apple, zucchini, cauliflower, broccoli, pear, spinach, lamb, chicken, beef, turkey, beans, lentils*

Mashed potatoes are a terrific finger food (so much fun!) for brave parents who don't mind cleaning up the mess. But, of course, you can also serve them on a spoon.

• •

1 Peel the potatoes or sweet potatoes. Poke them several times with a fork.

2 Pour the water into the multi-cooker. Add the potatoes (no need to chop them). Lock the lid and set to cook on high pressure for 15 minutes. When cooking is complete, press "Cancel" and carefully quick-release the pressure.

3 Remove the lid and let the potatoes cool slightly. Using an immersion blender or potato masher, blend or mash until smooth. (Do not overmix potatoes with the immersion blender, or they will become gummy.)

Makes about 3 cups

SLOW COOK IT: Place 4 chopped peeled large potatoes or sweet potatoes and ½ cup water in a slow cooker. Cover and cook on High for 3 to 4 hours, or until tender. Blend or mash until smooth.

Potato Nutrition per serving (2 tablespoons): 20 calories; 0g protein; 0g fat (0g sat. fat); 4g carbohydrates; 1g fiber; 0g sugars; 5mg sodium; 3mg calcium; 0.2mg iron; 115mg potassium; 3mg vitamin C; 2IU vitamin A

Sweet Potato Nutrition per serving (2 tablespoons): 24 calories; 0g protein; 0g fat (0g sat. fat); 6g carbohydrates; 1g fiber; 1g sugars; 16mg sodium; 9mg calcium; 0.2mg iron; 96mg potassium; 1mg vitamin C; 4,022IU vitamin A

RUTABAGA ❄ ㉚

Rutabaga may not be the most common root veggie on our tables, but it's worth cooking up a batch. The flavor is just a touch bitter, like a turnip, and it's a stellar companion to other vegetable and meat purées. Be sure to remove all the waxy skin. I've found that the easiest method is to cut off the top and bottom, sit the rutabaga flat on a cutting board, and then use a vegetable peeler in a circular motion, turning the root as I peel.

¾ cup water

1 rutabaga (2½ to 3 pounds), peeled and cut into roughly 2 x ½-inch sticks

Flavor Kick: *Melt a couple of tablespoons of unsalted butter into the finished purée for a creamy play on mashed potatoes.*

Purée Playdates: *Zucchini, cauliflower, broccoli, pea, spinach, lentil, bean, lamb, chicken, beef, turkey*

1 Pour the water into the multi-cooker. Add the rutabaga. Lock the lid and set to cook on high pressure for 6 minutes. When cooking is complete, press "Cancel" and carefully quick-release the pressure.

2 Remove the lid and let the rutabaga cool slightly. Using an immersion blender, blend until smooth.

Makes 5 cups

SLOW COOK IT: Place 1 chopped peeled rutabaga and 1 cup water in a slow cooker. Cover and cook on Low for 6 to 8 hours, or until tender, adding more water after 3 hours if the mixture seems dry. Blend until smooth.

Nutrition per serving (2 tablespoons): 13 calories; 0g protein; 0g fat (0g sat. fat); 3g carbohydrates; 1g fiber; 2g sugars; 4mg sodium; 15mg calcium; 0.2mg iron; 104mg potassium; 9mg vitamin C; 1IU vitamin A

SALMON, COD, OR OTHER THICK FISH FILLETS

Nonstick cooking spray

½ cup water

Two 6- to 8-ounce skinless fish fillets, any bones removed

Purée Playdates: *Apple, zucchini, potato, broccoli, cauliflower, lentil, spinach*

Make It a Finger Food: *Transfer the cooked fish to a plate to cool. When it's cool enough to handle, flake it with a fork.*

Go fish! Salmon is one of the healthiest foods you can offer your baby, thanks to its abundance of protein and brain-building omega-3 fatty acids. White-fleshed fish like cod are high in protein and are good sources of several B vitamins like niacin, B_6 and B_{12}. To find any bones in the fish before cooking, run your fingers lightly over both sides of each fillet. If you feel any bones, pull them out with tweezers. To be safe, do a quick visual check for bones after cooking and remove any stragglers.

1 Spray the walls of the cooker with cooking spray. Pour the water into the multi-cooker. Add the fish. Lock the lid and set to cook on high pressure for 3 to 4 minutes, depending on the thickness of the fillets. When cooking is complete, press "Cancel" and carefully quick-release the pressure.

2 Remove the lid and let the fish cool slightly. Using an immersion blender, blend until smooth.

Makes 2 cups

SLOW COOK IT: Place 1½ pounds skinless fish fillets and ¼ cup water in a slow cooker. Cover and cook on Low for 2 to 3 hours, or until the fish flakes easily with a fork. Blend until smooth.

Salmon Nutrition per serving (2 tablespoons purée): 40 calories; 6g protein; 2g fat (0g sat. fat); 0g carbohydrates; 0g fiber; 0g sugars; 13mg sodium; 4mg calcium; 0.2mg iron; 139mg potassium; 0mg vitamin C; 11IU vitamin A

Cod Nutrition per serving (2 tablespoons purée): 20 calories; 4g protein; 0g fat (0g sat. fat); 0g carbohydrates; 0g fiber; 0g sugars; 86mg sodium; 2mg calcium; 0.1mg iron; 67mg potassium; 0mg vitamin C; 2IU vitamin A

Flavor Kick: Add a squeeze of fresh lemon juice to the finished purée or flaked fish.

baby-led feeding and finger foods

Baby-led feeding is my take on baby-led weaning, a method of starting solids that sprang up in the UK and has been gaining popularity around the world over the last few years. With baby-led feeding, there is no spooning of purées into your baby's mouth. Instead, babies self-feed from the earliest days of starting solids, picking up small bites or larger sticks of food to explore and (hopefully!) eat.

The benefits of baby-led feeding are many. Babies practice their fine motor skills, develop independence, and learn to recognize their own hunger and satiety cues. They stop eating when they've had enough, not when the spoon stops coming. Self-feeding also allows babies to really explore foods, touching, smelling, tasting, and, yes, playing with their meals. Plus, babies who are self-feeding can join family meals sooner, eating modified versions of what the rest of the family is enjoying. And best of all, babies who self-feed may be less choosy as they get older.

What makes a safe finger food? Shape and texture are key. Foods should be cut into small chickpea-size pieces or into sticks the length and width of an adult's pinky finger. In terms of texture, foods should be soft, but not so soft that they turn into mush as soon as your baby palms them. You should be able to squish foods between your thumb and forefinger with gentle pressure.

I am a big advocate of including both finger foods and purées in a beginning eater's diet, rather than an all-or-nothing approach. This helps ensure that babies get the necessary amounts of essential nutrients and also learn to manage a variety of textures, including soft purées. In the end, I think the most important aspect of a baby's diet is variety.

If you do choose to start exclusively with purées, be sure to move on to chunkier textures as soon as your baby is able to manage them. Children who stay with purées longer are often choosier during their toddler years.

And if you are spoon-feeding, consider offering finger foods at the same meal, either before or after the purée. Excellent starter finger foods include small chunks of banana, small chunks of avocado, small soft pieces of other fruits and vegetables, Cheerios, and Bamba, Israeli peanut puff snacks (a great way to introduce peanuts!).

SPAGHETTI SQUASH

Save this one for more advanced eaters, since these squash strands aren't completely soft—they do have a tiny bit of bite. Older babies should be able to easily gum them into submission.

1 cup water

1 smallish spaghetti squash (2½ pounds), halved lengthwise and seeded

1 Pour the water into the multi-cooker. Place the metal steamer rack that came with the multi-cooker into the pot. Set the squash on the rack. Lock the lid and set to cook on high pressure for 10 minutes. When cooking is complete, press "Cancel" and carefully quick-release the pressure.

2 Remove the lid and transfer the squash to a large bowl or cutting board to cool; discard the liquid in the cooker.

3 When the squash is cool enough to handle, use a fork to scrape the flesh from the skin into strands; discard the skin. Serve as a finger food.

Makes about 3 cups

Flavor Kick: *Coat the cooked squash with a little marinara sauce.*

SLOW COOK IT: Place the squash halves and ½ cup water in a 5- or 6-quart slow cooker. Cover and cook on High for 2 to 3 hours, or until tender. Scrape out the squash strands as directed above.

Nutrition per serving (2 tablespoons): 12 calories; 0g protein; 0g fat (0g sat. fat); 3g carbohydrates; 1g fiber; 1g sugars; 7mg sodium; 9mg calcium; 0.12mg iron; 41mg potassium; 1mg vitamin C; 45IU vitamin A

GREEK-STYLE YOGURT

2 quarts whole milk
(½ gallon)

2 tablespoons plain full-fat Greek yogurt (with live active cultures)

Making yogurt in a multi-cooker is a four-step process, but very straightforward: scald the milk to sterilize it, cool the milk, incubate it with a yogurt starter (your favorite plain store-bought yogurt), then strain it. The total time is about 12 hours, but the active time is probably only 15 minutes.

Why bother? Two reasons. First, this recipe makes 4 cups of yogurt from just ½ gallon of milk; that's a huge cost savings over buying the same amount of yogurt, a win if your family eats a lot of the stuff. Second, it's so easy to do, and you'll get a real sense of accomplishment out of knowing that you *made yogurt*.

Note: I developed this recipe using the Instant Pot's "Yogurt" function. If you're using another model of multi-cooker, the process will be similar, but consult the owner's manual for specific directions.

• •

1 Pour the milk into the multi-cooker. Lock the lid with the pressure valve set to Sealing. On the Instant Pot, press the "Yogurt" button and then "Adjust" until "Boil" appears. The cycle should run for about 30 minutes.

2 When the cycle is over, remove the lid and use pot holders to remove the pot from the cooker. Let the milk cool at room temperature to 110°F, stirring every 15 minutes or so; this will take about 1 hour. The easiest way to gauge the temperature is to use a candy thermometer. If you don't have a candy thermometer, you can test the milk by feel.

You want it to be just slightly, noticeably warm, almost body temperature. If the milk is too hot, the yogurt starter will die when you add it. If it's too cool, the starter won't be activated.

3 Once the milk has cooled to 110°F, whisk in the Greek yogurt.

4 Return the pot to the cooker. Lock the lid with the pressure valve set to Venting. Press the "Yogurt" button and then "Adjust" until "Normal" appears. Set the time to 8 hours.

5 Meanwhile, place a large colander over a large bowl. Line the colander with a couple of layers of cheesecloth or a clean tea towel. When cooking is complete, remove the lid and, using pot holders, remove the pot from the multi-cooker. Pour the yogurt from the pot into the lined colander. Let sit at room temperature for 1 hour, then cover loosely with plastic wrap and refrigerate for another 1 to 3 hours, depending on how thick you like your yogurt.

6 Transfer the strained yogurt from the colander to a storage container. Whisk until smooth, then cover and refrigerate for up to 5 days. The liquid left in the bowl is whey. Discard it or transfer it to an airtight container and refrigerate it to use in smoothies (it's high in protein).

Makes about 4 cups

Serve It Up: *Offer your baby plain yogurt, or combine it with virtually any fruit or vegetable purée.*

• •

Nutrition per serving (2 tablespoons): 38 calories; 2g protein; 2g fat (1g sat. fat); 3g carbohydrates; 0g fiber; 0g sugars; 33mg sodium; 76mg calcium; 0mg iron; 1mg potassium; 1mg vitamin C; 76IU vitamin A

ZUCCHINI AND ❄ ⏱ SUMMER SQUASH

½ cup water

3 medium zucchini or summer squash (about 1½ pounds), trimmed and cut into 1-inch chunks

Flavor Kick: *Crush some dried oregano between your fingers and stir it into the finished purée.*

Purée Playdates: *Potato, sweet potato, chicken, salmon, beef, cauliflower, broccoli, carrot, beans, lentils*

Zucchini and yellow squash are full of water, so this purée is on the thinner side. Bulk it up by mixing it with a thicker purée like potato or stirring in some baby cereal.

1 Pour the water into the multi-cooker. Add the squash chunks. Lock the lid and set to cook on high pressure for 2 minutes. When cooking is complete, press "Cancel" and carefully quick-release the pressure.

2 Remove the lid and let the squash cool slightly. Using an immersion blender, blend until smooth.

Makes 2½ cups

SLOW COOK IT: Chop 4 medium zucchini or summer squash (or a combo) into thick rounds and place them in a slow cooker with ½ cup water. Cover and cook on Low for 2 hours, or until tender. Blend until smooth.

Nutrition per serving (2 tablespoons): 6 calories; 0g protein; 0g fat (0g sat. fat); 1g carbohydrates; 0g fiber; 1g sugars; 3mg sodium; 6mg calcium; 0.1mg iron; 89mg potassium; 6mg vitamin C; 68IU vitamin A

LEFTOVER-PURÉE PANCAKES ✋ ❄ 30

If you make purées for your baby, chances are you'll have some leftovers in the freezer when he moves past them. Or, if he's eating both purées and finger foods, you might want to vary the offerings from one day to the next without starting from scratch. Either way, these tender, nutritious patties are the solution. You can use any fruit or vegetable purée.

1 large egg

1 cup fruit or vegetable purée

¼ cup panko bread crumbs, plus more as needed

2 tablespoons olive oil

1 Crack the egg into a medium bowl and lightly beat it with a fork. Add the purée and panko and stir to combine. If the mixture seems too thin, add a little more panko.

2 In a medium skillet, heat 1 tablespoon olive oil over medium-high heat. Drop the batter by the tablespoon into the pan, making sure not to crowd the pan. Cook until browned on both sides, about 3 minutes per side. Transfer the finished pancakes to a plate and repeat with the remaining 1 tablespoon olive oil to cook the remaining batter.

Makes about 10 pancakes (1 pancake per serving)

FRESH FROM THE FREEZER

Green peas and spinach are two classic baby foods, but they are too delicate to cook well in a multi-cooker or slow cooker. Instead, start with frozen and cook them in the microwave or on the stovetop for super-easy blends. Rest assured that frozen vegetables are just as healthy as their fresh counterparts. They're picked at the height of ripeness and frozen immediately, so no nutrients are lost.

PEAS

Cook one 10-ounce package frozen peas according to the package directions. Drain the peas and transfer them to a standard blender. Add 1 to 2 tablespoons water. Blend until smooth, adding more water as needed for a smoother purée.

Nutrition per serving (2 tablespoons): 19 calories; 1g protein; 0g fat (0g sat. fat); 3g carbohydrates; 1g fiber; 1g sugars; 1mg sodium; 6mg calcium; 0mg iron; 58mg potassium; 9mg vitamin C; 181IU vitamin A

SPINACH

Cook one 10-ounce package frozen chopped spinach according to the package directions; do not drain the spinach. Let cool for 10 minutes, then transfer the spinach and its liquid to a standard blender. Blend until smooth, adding water as needed for a smoother purée.

Nutrition per serving (2 tablespoons): 8 calories; 1g protein; 0g fat (0g sat. fat); 1g carbohydrates; 1g fiber; 0g sugars; 19mg sodium; 33mg calcium; 1mg iron; 98mg potassium; 1mg vitamin C; 3,027IU vitamin A

gagging and choking

Many parents are reluctant to give their babies finger foods for fear of the baby choking. But you'll be amazed at how adept your baby is at chewing and managing foods in his mouth. Making sure that foods are the appropriate size and texture (as described on page 76) is key.

Your baby may gag when he is learning to eat. This is very common, and while scary for parents and sometimes for baby, it's actually your baby's natural defense mechanism against choking. As babies get older, around eight or nine months, the gagging reflex shifts closer to the back of the tongue and gagging occurs less frequently.

Frequent gagging can be distressing for babies, however, and, in more extreme cases, can cause them to vomit or lose interest in eating. Talk with your pediatrician if gagging seems to impede your baby's enjoyment of mealtime. Excessive gagging might signal that your baby isn't quite ready for certain textures yet. Take a step back and try again in a week or two. All babies are different, and feeding isn't a race!

Choking is a real hazard, however. Make sure to always stay with your baby when he's eating. Don't offer choking hazards such as whole grapes, cut-up hot dogs, gobs of nut butter, whole nuts, popcorn, or hard candy. Know the signs of choking: weak coughing or crying, flapping or waving hands, staring with an open mouth, clutching the throat, and lips and under eye areas turning blue. Take an infant and child CPR class to familiarize yourself with how to help your baby if he does choke.

ALL BABIES ARE DIFFERENT, AND FEEDING ISN'T A RACE!

banana

Happily, not all baby food needs to be cooked.

strawberries

pineapp

avocado

prunes

blueberries

NO-COOK PURÉES

AVOCADO

Mash ¼ avocado until smooth.

BANANA

Choose a ripe banana. Mash with a fork until smooth.

BLUEBERRIES

Purée in a standard blender, then strain through a fine-mesh sieve.

PINEAPPLE

Purée pineapple chunks in a standard blender.

PRUNES

Soak in hot water for 20 minutes. Blend the prunes with enough
of the water to make a smooth purée.

STRAWBERRIES

Blend in a standard blender for a perfectly smooth purée, or
mash with a potato masher for more texture. Be sure to start with ripe, not hard,
strawberries for the best texture and flavor.

NO-COOK FINGER FOODS

To be safe for baby, finger foods need to be soft enough to mash between your thumb and forefinger with gentle pressure. And they should either be cut into small thumbnail-size pieces or larger pinky-finger-size sticks.

AVOCADO WEDGES

BANANA PIECES OR BANANA IN ITS PEEL

SHREDDED CHEESE

SMALL, SOFT PIECES OF STRAWBERRY

SMASHED BLUEBERRIES

SMASHED RASPBERRIES

CHAPTER THREE
NEXT
STEPS
(8 months and up)

AS YOUR BABY GETS **OLDER,** SHE'S READY FOR **MORE!**

All the eating practice your baby has had over the past couple of months is likely paying off. As her eating skills develop, she'll be ready for more complex dishes and foods with additional texture. It's okay to still spoon-feed a purée or two during this stage, but if your baby is capable of self-feeding, make that her main mode at the table. She can self-feed with her fingers or a spoon. You can even give her a head start by preloading a spoon. Eating with utensils takes time, but let her watch you expertly wielding your spoon and give her plenty of opportunities to practice. You'll be surprised at her coordination.

Yuck to Yum

Remember, it's okay if your baby doesn't like a food on the first go. Some gentle encouragement to try a new food is okay, but if she's not interested, just move on to another option and try the less-liked food again the next day and the day after. Then freeze the leftovers and try them again the following week or even the next month. For many babies and most toddlers, a big component of liking foods is being familiar with them. Children can become familiar with foods by tasting them, of course, but also by touching, smelling, playing with, and even licking them.

Raise a Kitchen Buddy

This is also a great age to have baby nearby while you're cooking. If she's game, secure her in her high chair where she can watch you cook. If you're making green beans, offer her a few to explore. Give her a play-by-play of what you're up to ("Now I'm stirring together the spices for the beef"), and let her hear the sounds and smell the aromas of the kitchen. She won't be ready to don an apron just yet, but she'll begin to make the connection about where her food comes from, and before you know it, she'll be ready to help stir and mash.

Age It Up

Many of the recipes in this chapter have an "Age It Up" note with instructions on how to transition the dish from baby food to family food. Sometimes it's adding salt to boost flavor; other times I offer serving suggestions for rounding out the recipe into a full meal.

PEELS-ON ❄ ⓷⓪ APPLESAUCE

4 Gala apples (2 pounds), cored and sliced

½ cup water

1 tablespoon unsalted butter

Pinch of ground cardamom

Pinch of ground cinnamon

Leaving the skins on gives this apple purée a subtle pink hue. This is one recipe to keep in your repertoire even when your baby is all grown up.

1 Place the apple slices in the multi-cooker. Pour in the water. Lock the lid and set to cook on high pressure for 5 minutes. When cooking is complete, press "Cancel" and carefully quick-release the pressure.

2 Remove the lid and let the apples cool slightly. Using an immersion blender, blend until smooth. Stir in the butter, cardamom, and cinnamon.

Makes about 2½ cups

SLOW COOK IT: Place the ingredients in a slow cooker. Cover and cook on Low for 4 to 6 hours, or until the apples are very tender. Blend until smooth.

Nutrition per serving (¼ cup): 55 calories; 0g protein; 1g fat (1g sat. fat); 11g carbohydrates; 2g fiber; 8g sugars; 1mg sodium; 6mg calcium; 0.1mg iron; 86mg potassium; 0mg vitamin C; 58IU vitamin A

RAPID ❄ 🕥 RATATOUILLE

I will not claim that this colorful dish is anywhere close to traditional ratatouille. But it boasts many of the same vegetables, and it cooks in a fraction of the time. Stir in some cooked quinoa to make this a meal.

. . . .

1 Pour the water into the multi-cooker. Add the zucchini, bell pepper, and eggplant. Lock the lid and set to cook on high pressure for 2 minutes. When cooking is complete, press "Cancel" and carefully quick-release the pressure.

2 Stir in the tomatoes, olive oil, and herbes de Provence (if using). Let the ratatouille cool slightly. Using an immersion blender, blend until smooth, or, for a meal with more texture, mash gently with a potato masher.

Makes 4½ cups

SLOW COOK IT: Skip the water and don't drain the tomatoes. Place all the ingredients in a slow cooker. Cover and cook on High for 2 to 3 hours, or until the vegetables are very tender. Blend or mash as described in Step 2.

Nutrition per serving (¼ cup): 28 calories; 1g protein; 1g fat (0g sat. fat); 4g carbohydrates; 1g fiber; 3g sugars; 52mg sodium; 26mg calcium; 0.4mg iron; 101mg potassium; 16mg vitamin C; 307IU vitamin A

¼ cup water

1 medium zucchini (about 1½ pounds), trimmed and cut into 1-inch chunks

1 red bell pepper, cored and cut into chunks

1 medium eggplant (about 1 pound), trimmed and cut into 1-inch chunks

One 28-ounce can diced tomatoes, drained

1 tablespoon olive oil

½ teaspoon herbes de Provence (optional)

GO GREEN
PURÉE

This purée isn't perfectly smooth—just what you want for more advanced eaters. Frozen peas can stand in for the edamame.

· ·

1 Set the multi-cooker to Sauté. Melt the butter in the pot, then add the leek and cook, stirring, until just tender, about 5 minutes. If the leek begins browning, add a tablespoon or so of water.

2 Pour the water into the pot. Add the asparagus and edamame. Lock the lid and set to cook on high pressure for 3 minutes. When cooking is complete, press "Cancel" and carefully quick-release the pressure.

3 Let the mixture cool slightly. Using an immersion blender, blend until smoothish.

Makes about 1¼ cups

· ·

Nutrition per serving (¼ cup): 82 calories; 4g protein; 5g fat (3g sat. fat); 6g carbohydrates; 3g fiber; 2g sugars; 6mg sodium; 44mg calcium; 2mg iron; 201mg potassium; 8mg vitamin C; 991IU vitamin A

2 tablespoons unsalted butter

1 leek, white and light green parts only, sliced (about ½ cup)

½ cup water

1 bunch asparagus (about 1 pound), woody ends snapped off

½ cup frozen shelled edamame

AUTUMN ❄
ROOT VEGGIE MASH

5 small turnips, peeled and cut into 1-inch pieces

3 carrots, peeled and cut into 1-inch pieces

2 parsnips, peeled, halved, woody cores removed, and cut into 1-inch pieces

1 medium golden beet, peeled and cut into ½-inch pieces

½ cup water

1 tablespoon olive oil

2 teaspoons apple cider vinegar

Root vegetables take on a sweetness when cooked, so chances are, your baby will enjoy this nutritious veggie mélange. The beets take the longest to cook, so be sure to cut them into smaller pieces.

1   Place the turnips, carrots, parsnips, beet, and water in the multi-cooker. Lock the lid and set to cook on high pressure for 11 minutes. When cooking is complete, press "Cancel" and carefully quick-release the pressure.

2   Add the olive oil and vinegar. Let the vegetables cool slightly. Mash with a potato masher for a coarser dish or blend until smooth using an immersion blender.

Makes 3 cups

SLOW COOK IT: Place the turnips, carrots, parsnips, beet, and water in a slow cooker. Cover and cook on Low for 6 hours, or until the vegetables are very tender. Continue with the recipe at Step 2.

Nutrition per serving (¼ cup): 43 calories; 1g protein; 1g fat (0g sat. fat); 8g carbohydrates; 2g fiber; 3g sugars; 35mg sodium; 22mg calcium; 0.3mg iron; 205mg potassium; 10mg vitamin C; 2,550IU vitamin A

SQUASH AND PEPPER
PURÉE ❄ 🕒

You can spoon-feed this purée to your baby, or toss it with pasta for a satisfying finger food.

½ cup water

3 medium zucchini or summer squash (about 1½ pounds), trimmed and cut into 1-inch chunks

1 red or orange bell pepper, cored and cut into chunks

2 tablespoons grated Parmesan cheese

¼ teaspoon dried oregano

1 Pour the water into the multi-cooker. Add the squash and bell pepper. Lock the lid and set to cook on high pressure for 2 minutes. When cooking is complete, press "Cancel" and carefully quick-release the pressure.

2 Remove the lid and let the vegetables cool slightly. Using an immersion blender, blend until smooth. Stir in the Parmesan and oregano.

Makes 3 cups

SLOW COOK IT: Combine the squash, bell pepper, and ¼ cup water in a slow cooker. Cover and cook on High for 3 to 4 hours, or until the vegetables are very tender. Blend until smooth. Stir in the Parmesan and oregano.

Nutrition per serving (¼ cup): 17 calories; 1g protein; 1g fat (0g sat. fat); 2g carbohydrates; 1g fiber; 2g sugars; 21mg sodium; 22mg calcium; 0.3mg iron; 170mg potassium; 23mg vitamin C; 433IU vitamin A

SESAME PEARS ❄ ㉚

6 ripe Bartlett pears (about 2 pounds), halved and cored (do not peel)

¼ cup water

2 tablespoons tahini (sesame seed paste)

Black sesame seeds, for garnish (optional)

Tahini, or sesame seed paste, adds a nutty richness to this sweet purée. Spoon-feed it, or offer it to your baby on a preloaded spoon.

• •

1 Place the pears in the multi-cooker. Pour in the water. Lock the lid and set to cook on high pressure for 3 minutes. When cooking is complete, press "Cancel" and carefully quick-release the pressure.

2 Remove the lid and, using pot holders, remove the pot from the cooker. Carefully drain off most of the liquid, leaving a tablespoon or two. Using an immersion blender, blend until smooth. Stir in the tahini. Serve topped with sesame seeds, if desired.

Makes about 2 cups

> **SLOW COOK IT:** Place the pears and water in a slow cooker. Cover and cook on Low for 3 hours, or until tender, stirring once after 1 hour. Continue with the recipe as described in Step 2.

Nutrition per serving (¼ cup): 87 calories; 1g protein; 2g fat (0g sat. fat); 18g carbohydrates; 4g fiber; 11g sugars; 6mg sodium; 26mg calcium; 1mg iron; 147mg potassium; 5mg vitamin C; 31IU vitamin A

HERBY ❄ ㉚ RED LENTILS

Fiber- and folate-rich red lentils cook so quickly and thoroughly, they basically purée themselves. This is one of my favorite stews to serve eaters of any age. To make it a meal for the whole family, serve it with bread or crackers and a green salad.

Stir together all the ingredients in a multi-cooker. Lock the lid and set to cook on high pressure for 5 minutes. When cooking is complete, press "Cancel" and let the pressure release naturally.

Makes 2 cups

SLOW COOK IT: Combine 2 cups dried red lentils, 5 cups water, 1 cup grated carrots (3 or 4 carrots), 2 teaspoons finely chopped fresh rosemary, and 2 teaspoons finely chopped fresh oregano in a slow cooker. Cover and cook on Low for 6 to 7 hours, or until the lentils and carrots are tender.

Nutrition per serving (¼ cup): 88 calories; 7g protein; 1g fat (0g sat. fat); 15g carbohydrates; 4g fiber; 1g sugars; 9mg sodium; 16mg calcium; 1mg iron; 240mg potassium; 0mg vitamin C; 1,153IU vitamin A

1 cup dried red lentils, rinsed

½ cup grated carrot
(1 or 2 carrots)

2 cups water

1 teaspoon finely chopped
fresh rosemary

1 teaspoon finely chopped
fresh oregano

Age It Up: *Add ¾ teaspoon kosher salt before cooking.*

SWEET-AND-SAVORY ✋ ❄️
LAMB STEW

½ pound boneless lamb stew meat, trimmed of fat and cut into 1-inch pieces

1 large carrot, peeled and cut into small pieces

2 tablespoons golden raisins

½ cup cooked or canned chickpeas (rinsed and drained if canned)

½ cup low-sodium beef broth

With its chunks of meat, carrots, raisins, and chickpeas, this hearty main is ideal for self-feeding, but it can also be puréed or mashed for spoon-feeding.

1 Combine all the ingredients in the multi-cooker. Lock the lid and set to cook on high pressure for 30 minutes. When cooking is complete, press "Cancel" and carefully quick-release the pressure.

2 Use a slotted spoon to transfer the lamb mixture to a bowl or storage container, reserving the cooking liquid if puréeing. Before serving as a finger food, gently smash the chickpeas, and chop or shred the meat. If puréeing, blend the lamb mixture with the reserved cooking liquid in a standard blender or with an immersion blender.

Makes 2 cups

SLOW COOK IT: Double the recipe, using 1 cup beef broth and 1 cup water. Place all of the ingredients in a slow cooker. Cover and cook on Low for 6 to 8 hours, or until the lamb is tender.

Nutrition per serving (¼ cup): 66 calories; 7g protein; 2g fat (1g sat. fat); 5g carbohydrates; 1g fiber; 2g sugars; 52mg sodium; 11mg calcium; 0.9mg iron; 152mg potassium; 1mg vitamin C; 1,277IU vitamin A

JUST ✋❄ MEATBALLS

These are basic nuggets of meaty goodness, nothing fancy, but an easy and fun way to offer your baby protein, iron, and zinc. Gussy up the meatballs by adding minced garlic, some grated Parm, or lemon zest. You could also sub in ground beef or ground chicken for the turkey.

½ cup rolled oats

1 large egg

1 pound 93% lean ground turkey

1 teaspoon dried oregano

Freshly ground black pepper

½ cup low-sodium chicken broth

1 In a blender or mini food processor, pulse the oats until finely chopped.

2 In a large bowl, beat the egg with a fork. Add the ground turkey, oregano, a few twists of pepper, and the ground oats. Mix until combined.

3 Pour the broth into the multi-cooker. Form the meat mixture into about 15 Ping-Pong-ball-size meatballs and place them in the broth. Lock the lid and set to cook on high pressure for 5 minutes. When cooking is complete, press "Cancel" and let the pressure release naturally for 10 minutes, then carefully quick-release any remaining pressure.

Age It Up: *Add ¾ teaspoon kosher salt to the meat mixture before forming the meatballs.*

Makes about 15 meatballs

> **SLOW COOK IT:** Spray a slow cooker insert with nonstick cooking spray. Place the meatballs in the slow cooker and add the broth. Cover and cook on Low for 6 hours.

Nutrition per meatball: 51 calories; 5g protein; 2g fat (1g sat. fat); 2g carbohydrates; 0g fiber; 0g sugars; 23mg sodium; 7mg calcium; 1.5mg iron; 60mg potassium; 0mg vitamin C; 35IU vitamin A

TROPICAL ✋ ❄ ⏲ FRUIT SALAD

Babies love fruit, but sometimes fresh fruit isn't quite soft enough for self-feeding. One minute in the pressure cooker leaves tropical fruit like papaya and mango just the right texture. For an even simpler salad, skip the strawberries and kiwi.

1 cup water

4 cups chopped (about ½-inch cubes) papaya and/or mango (from 1 papaya and 1 to 2 mangoes for an even mix)

½ cup chopped strawberries

½ cup chopped peeled kiwifruit

1 Pour the water into the multi-cooker. Place a metal steamer basket into the pot. Add the papaya and/or mango cubes. Lock the lid and set to cook on high pressure for 1 minute. When cooking is complete, press "Cancel" and carefully quick-release the pressure.

2 Add the strawberries and/or kiwi. Cover the pot with the lid, but do not lock it. Let sit for 3 minutes.

3 Use a slotted spoon to transfer the fruit salad to a serving dish or storage containers.

Makes 4 cups

Nutrition per serving (¼ cup): 18 calories; 0g protein; 0g fat (0g sat. fat); 5g carbohydrates; 1g fiber; 3g sugars; 3mg sodium; 9mg calcium; 0.1mg iron; 80mg potassium; 27mg vitamin C; 334IU vitamin A

Nutrition Note: *Papaya, mango, strawberry, and kiwi are all rich in vitamin C, an essential nutrient for tissue formation.*

TURMERIC CAULIFLOWER

2 tablespoons olive oil

¾ cup chopped yellow onion

2 garlic cloves, sliced

1 teaspoon ground turmeric

¼ teaspoon ground ginger

Pinch ground cinnamon

½ cup water

4 cups cauliflower florets (about ½ medium head)

½ cup canned diced fire-roasted tomatoes, with their juices

Age It Up: *Add ½ teaspoon kosher salt with the spices. Serve over rice.*

Cutting the cauliflower into florets with short stem "handles" makes it easier for babies to pick up the veggie with the palm of their hands. For eaters who have developed their pincer grasp—meaning they can pick up foods with their thumb and forefinger—chop the cooked cauliflower into smaller chunks for self-feeding.

1 Set the multi-cooker to Sauté. When the pot is hot, add the olive oil. Add the onion and cook, stirring frequently, until just tender, 3 to 5 minutes. Add the garlic, turmeric, ginger, and cinnamon. Cook for another minute.

2 Pour the water into the multi-cooker. Add the cauliflower and tomatoes. Lock the lid and set to cook on high pressure for 1 minute. When cooking is complete, press "Cancel" and carefully quick-release the pressure.

3 Remove the lid and let the cauliflower cool. Serve as a finger food.

Makes about 3 cups

Nutrition per serving (¼ cup): 31 calories; 1g protein; 2g fat (0g sat. fat); 2g carbohydrates; 1g fiber; 1g sugars; 29mg sodium; 29mg calcium; 0.3mg iron; 85mg potassium; 12mg vitamin C; 17IU vitamin A

BANANA ⊙ ❄ ③⓪ QUINOA

1 cup uncooked quinoa, rinsed if necessary (check the package directions)

1 cup water

1½ cups unsweetened nondairy milk, such as almond or coconut (see Note)

1 ripe banana, mashed

¼ teaspoon ground cinnamon

Nutrition Note: *This recipe calls for nondairy milk, since babies should avoid large quantities of cow's milk. (A little dairy is okay in cooking or baked goods, but since this recipe calls for over a cup, stick with nondairy.) Today, there are more nondairy milks at the supermarket than ever. Make sure you choose an unsweetened variety.*

Full disclosure: The bottom of the multi-cooker pot may scorch a bit as you're simmering this baby-pleasing dish. If you let it soak for an hour or so, cleanup will be easier. Permission to procrastinate: granted!

1 Combine the quinoa and water in the multi-cooker and stir. Lock the lid and set to cook on high pressure for 1 minute. When cooking is complete, press "Cancel" and let the pressure release naturally.

2 Remove the lid and set the multi-cooker to Sauté. Add the nondairy milk. Simmer, stirring frequently, until the milk has been mostly absorbed and the quinoa is creamy, about 5 minutes. Press "Cancel."

3 Stir in the mashed banana and cinnamon.

Makes about 3 cups

Nutrition per serving (¼ cup): 60 calories; 3g protein; 1g fat (0g sat. fat); 11g carbohydrates; 1g fiber; 1g sugars; 19mg sodium; 31mg calcium; 1.3mg iron; 142mg potassium; 1mg vitamin C; 163IU vitamin A

COCONUT ❄ RICE PORRIDGE

Serve this creamy porridge as-is any time of day for a filling, whole-grain meal. Or stir in a tablespoon or two of finely chopped fruit, fruit purée, or vegetable purée. For more advanced eaters, top the porridge with toasted shredded coconut and some small, soft pieces of fruit.

¾ cup uncooked brown basmati rice

¼ cup uncooked white basmati rice

One 13.5-ounce can coconut milk

3½ cups water

1 Combine the brown rice, white rice, coconut milk, and water in the multi-cooker and stir. Lock the lid and set to cook on high pressure for 30 minutes. When cooking is complete, press "Cancel" and let the pressure release naturally; this will take about 15 minutes.

2 Remove the lid and stir for a minute or two; the porridge will thicken.

Makes about 4½ cups

SLOW COOK IT: Place the brown basmati rice, white basmati rice, coconut milk, and 3½ cups water in a slow cooker. Cover and cook on Low for 5 to 6 hours.

Nutrition per serving (¼ cup): 72 calories; 1g protein; 4g fat (4g sat. fat); 8g carbohydrates; 0g fiber; 0g sugars; 7mg sodium; 1mg calcium; 0.3mg iron; 0mg potassium; 0mg vitamin C; 0IU vitamin A

CINNAMON ❄ REFRIED BEANS

2 cups dried pinto beans, rinsed

4 cups water

½ onion

2 garlic cloves

1 cinnamon stick

2 tablespoons canola oil

1 teaspoon ground cumin

Pinch of cayenne pepper (optional)

Age It Up: *Add 1 teaspoon kosher salt before cooking in Step 1, and an additional ½ teaspoon with the beans in Step 3.*

Let your baby feed these beans to herself with a spoon or spread them on a tortilla for her. For a tasty toddler lunch, roll up the beans and a little grated cheese in a tortilla. The cinnamon is subtle, but unexpectedly delicious.

1 Combine the beans, water, onion, garlic, and cinnamon stick in the multi-cooker. Lock the lid and set to cook on high pressure for 40 minutes. When cooking is complete, press "Cancel" and carefully quick-release the pressure.

2 Discard the cinnamon stick. Using a slotted spoon, transfer 3 cups of the beans, the onion half, and the garlic (if you can find it) to a large bowl. Set aside ½ cup of the cooking liquid in a separate small bowl. Transfer the remaining beans and cooking liquid to an airtight container and refrigerate or freeze for another use. (They will keep for up to 3 days in the fridge and 3 months in the freezer).

3 Rinse out the multi-cooker pot, wipe dry, and return to the multi-cooker. Set the multi-cooker to Sauté and pour in the canola oil. When the oil is hot, add the cumin and cayenne (if using) and cook for 1 minute. Add the 3 cups beans, onion, and garlic and mash the beans with a wooden spoon or a potato masher. Add ¼ cup of the reserved cooking liquid and cook until the beans are smoothish and creamy, about 3 minutes. If the beans seem too stiff, add more cooking liquid as needed.

Makes about 2½ cups

Nutrition per serving (¼ cup): 162 calories; 8g protein; 3g fat (0g sat. fat); 25g carbohydrates; 6g fiber; 1g sugars; 8mg sodium; 51mg calcium; 2.1mg iron; 553mg potassium; 3mg vitamin C; 0IU vitamin A

GARLICKY ✋ SPAGHETTI SQUASH

Feel free to use 3 cups leftover spaghetti squash in this recipe, or cook the squash the day before. Just make sure the liquid is squeezed out before sautéing.

•••

1 Pour the water into the multi-cooker. Place the metal rack that came with the multi-cooker in the pot. Set the squash on the rack. Lock the lid and set to cook on high pressure for 10 minutes. When cooking is complete, press "Cancel" and carefully quick-release the pressure.

2 Transfer the squash to a large bowl or cutting board to cool; discard the liquid in the multi-cooker. When the squash is cool enough to handle, use a fork to scrape the flesh from the skin into strands; discard the skin. Squeeze the strands to remove as much liquid as possible.

3 Wipe out the pot with a cloth or paper towel and return it to the multi-cooker. Set the multi-cooker to Sauté and pour in the olive oil. When the oil is hot, add the garlic and red pepper flakes (if using) and cook until the garlic is tender but not browned, about 5 minutes. Add the squash strands and a few twists of black pepper. Toss with tongs until the squash is warmed and coated with the olive oil. Press "Cancel." Serve topped with Parmesan, if desired.

Makes about 3 cups

••

Nutrition per serving (¼ cup): 54 calories; 1g protein; 4g fat (1g sat. fat); 5g carbohydrates; 1g fiber; 2g sugars; 14mg sodium; 19mg calcium; 0.3mg iron; 85mg potassium; 2mg vitamin C; 91IU vitamin A

1 cup water

1 smallish spaghetti squash (2½ pounds), halved lengthwise and seeded

3 tablespoons olive oil

3 garlic cloves, thinly sliced

Pinch of red pepper flakes (optional)

Freshly ground black pepper

Grated Parmesan cheese, for serving (optional)

Age It Up: *Add ¼ teaspoon kosher salt to the squash in step 3.*

•••••••••••••••••••••••••

SLOW COOK IT: Place the squash halves and ½ cup water in a 6-quart slow cooker. Cover and cook on High for 2 to 3 hours, or until tender. Proceed with the recipe as directed from step 2.

•••••••••••••••••••••••••

Flavor Kick: Add a few pinches of dried herbs, chopped fresh herbs, freshly ground black pepper, and/or grated Parmesan cheese to the egg mixture before cooking.

SIMPLE FRITTATA ✋ ❄️

When you make a frittata in a multi-cooker, the texture is perfectly soft, ideal for a beginning eater. Just let it cool, cut it into small pieces, and serve.

• •

1 Pour the water into the multi-cooker. Place the flat steamer rack that came with the multi-cooker in the pot. Spray a 1½-quart round soufflé dish with cooking spray. Place the dish in a silicone or aluminum foil sling (see page 22).

2 In a medium bowl, whisk together the eggs and milk. Pour them into the prepared soufflé dish.

3 Lower the dish in the sling onto the steamer rack. Lock the lid and set to cook on high pressure for 25 minutes. When cooking is complete, press "Cancel" and let the pressure release naturally for 10 minutes, then carefully quick-release any remaining pressure.

4 Using the sling, lift the dish out of the multi-cooker. Don't worry if there is liquid pooled on top of the eggs, just dab with a paper towel. Let the frittata cool before serving.

Makes 8 servings

• •

Nutrition per serving: 93 calories; 7g protein; 6g fat (3g sat. fat); 3g carbohydrates; 0g fiber; 3g sugars; 83mg sodium; 94mg calcium; 0.7mg iron; 158mg potassium; 0.7mg vitamin C; 277IU vitamin A

1½ cups water

Nonstick cooking spray

6 large eggs

½ cup whole milk

Age It Up: *Add ½ teaspoon kosher salt to the egg mixture before cooking.*

GOLDEN ❄ RICE AND PEAS

2 tablespoons coconut oil

1 cup chopped onion

1 teaspoon curry powder

½ teaspoon ground turmeric

4 cups water

1 cup dried yellow split peas, rinsed

¾ cup uncooked brown basmati rice

Juice of 1 lime

Age It Up: *Add 1½ teaspoons kosher salt with the water in step 2. For serving, sauté sliced garlic and red pepper flakes in butter, letting the butter turn golden brown. Drizzle the garlic butter on top of the rice and peas.*

You'll probably want to serve this mild and creamy dish on a preloaded spoon to save some cleanup, but don't be surprised if your baby wants to dive in with his hands.

1 Set the multi-cooker to Sauté. Melt the coconut oil in the pot. When the oil is hot, add the onion and cook, stirring frequently, until lightly browned, about 4 minutes. Add the curry powder and turmeric and cook, stirring, for another minute.

2 Stir in the water, split peas, and rice. Lock the lid and set to cook on high pressure for 22 minutes. When cooking is complete, press "Cancel" and let the pressure release naturally; this will take about 15 minutes.

3 Stir in the lime juice.

Makes 12 servings

Nutrition per serving (¼ cup): 60 calories; 3g protein; 2g fat (1g sat. fat); 10g carbohydrates; 3g fiber; 1g sugars; 44mg sodium; 7mg calcium; 0.4mg iron; 87mg potassium; 1mg vitamin C; 13IU vitamin A

BLUEBERRY ✋ ❄ BANANA BREAD

Although this bread does contain added sugar (generally a no-no to feed to babies), it's made mostly of bananas, blueberries, whole wheat flour, and eggs—all healthful, wholesome ingredients—with only a tiny amount of sugar (less than a teaspoon per serving). I trust you as a parent to decide when or whether to share a slightly sweet bread with your baby. Just don't go crazy and break out the chocolate bars just yet!

Nonstick cooking spray

1 cup whole-wheat flour

1 cup all-purpose flour

¾ teaspoon baking powder

¾ cup coconut oil or canola oil

2 large eggs

¼ cup packed dark brown sugar

1 teaspoon vanilla extract

3 very ripe bananas, mashed

½ cup fresh or frozen blueberries

1½ cups water

1 Spray a 1½-quart soufflé dish with cooking spray. In a large bowl, whisk together the whole-wheat flour, all-purpose flour, and baking powder. In a medium bowl or 4-cup liquid measuring cup, whisk together the oil, eggs, brown sugar, and vanilla. Stir the wet ingredients into the dry ingredients. Stir in the mashed bananas and blueberries. Transfer the batter to the prepared baking dish and cover with aluminum foil.

2 Pour the water into the multi-cooker. Place the metal rack that came with the multi-cooker into the pot. Place the covered soufflé dish in a silicone or aluminum foil sling (see page 22). Lower the dish on the sling onto the rack. Lock the lid and set to cook on high pressure for 50 minutes.

3 When cooking is complete, press "Cancel" and let the pressure release naturally for 10 minutes, then carefully quick-release the remaining pressure.

Age It Up: *Add ½ teaspoon kosher salt to the dry ingredients in step 1.*

(continues)

4 Using the sling, remove the soufflé dish from the multi-cooker and set it on a wire rack. Uncover the bread and let it cool in the dish for about 20 minutes. Remove the bread from the dish and let it cool completely on the rack.

Makes 18 servings

• •

Nutrition per serving: 166 calories; 3g protein; 10g fat (8g sat. fat); 18g carbohydrates; 2g fiber; 5g sugars; 36mg sodium; 13mg calcium; 0.7mg iron; 117mg potassium; 2mg vitamin C; 45IU vitamin A

GINGERED PEARS

Poached pears are an excellent finger food for the early days of baby-led feeding: tender enough for babies without teeth, but firm enough not to turn to mush in your baby's grasp.

1 Combine the pears, ginger, cinnamon stick, and water in the multi-cooker. Lock the lid and set to cook on high pressure for 3 to 4 minutes, depending on the size of the pears. When cooking is complete, press "Cancel" and carefully quick-release the pressure.

2 Transfer the pears to a plate or cutting board; discard the ginger, cinnamon stick, and liquid in the multi-cooker. Let cool before cutting into ½-inch-thick slices.

Makes 8 servings

> **SLOW COOK IT:** Place 3 peeled pears (no need to halve or core them), the ginger, cinnamon stick, and 1 cup water in a slow cooker. Cover and cook on High for 2 to 3 hours, or until the pears are tender when pierced with a knife but not too mushy to hold their shape. When cool enough, halve and core the pears, then slice.

Nutrition per serving (2 slices): 30 calories; 0g protein; 0g fat (0g sat. fat); 7g carbohydrates; 1g fiber; 5g sugars; 1mg sodium; 5mg calcium; 0.1mg iron; 48mg potassium; 2mg vitamin C; 13IU vitamin A

2 ripe but not too soft Bartlett pears, peeled, halved, and cored

1 ounce fresh ginger (about one 2½-inch piece), cut into coins (no need to peel)

1 cinnamon stick

½ cup water

Age It Up: *Cook the pears in unsweetened apple juice for extra flavor.*

BEET HUMMUS ❄

1 cup dried chickpeas, rinsed

3 cups water

1 teaspoon ground cumin

3 tablespoons fresh lemon juice

2 tablespoons olive oil

½ cup beet purée (see page 50)

Age It Up: *Add 1 teaspoon kosher salt to the chickpeas before cooking and more to taste while puréeing.*

You can stir virtually any vegetable purée into this protein-rich dip for added flavor and color, but I am partial to vibrant, earthy-sweet beets. Serve the hummus with a spoon for self-feeding, or steamed baby carrots or toast sticks for dipping.

1 Combine the chickpeas and water in the multi-cooker. Lock the lid and set to cook on high pressure for 40 minutes. When cooking is complete, press "Cancel" and let the pressure release naturally for 15 minutes, then carefully quick-release any remaining pressure.

2 Drain the chickpeas, reserving the cooking liquid. Transfer the chickpeas to a food processor, add 1 cup of the cooking liquid, and process until smooth, adding more cooking liquid as needed. Add the cumin, lemon juice, and olive oil and process until smooth and creamy. Add the beet purée and pulse to incorporate.

Makes 2½ cups

Nutrition per serving (¼ cup): 58 calories; 2g protein; 3g fat (0g sat. fat); 6g carbohydrates; 2g fiber; 2g sugars; 13mg sodium; 14mg calcium; 0.7mg iron; 94mg potassium; 3mg vitamin C; 9IU vitamin A

GET-YOUR-GREENS ✋ ❄️
QUINOA BITES

Packed with healthy spinach and quinoa, these are perfect on-the-go snacks for more advanced eaters and toddlers. Parmesan cheese can be used in place of the Asiago. If you only have one mini-muffin tin, bake the bites in batches.

∙∙∙

1 Preheat the oven to 375°F. Spray a mini-muffin tin with cooking spray.

2 Stir together the quinoa and water in the multi-cooker. Lock the lid and set to cook on high pressure for 1 minute. When cooking is complete, press "Cancel" and let the pressure release naturally.

3 Transfer the quinoa to a large bowl. Let cool for 10 minutes.

4 Add the egg whites, spinach, and cheese to the quinoa and stir to combine. Transfer the mixture to the prepared muffin tin, placing about 1 tablespoon in each cup and pressing down with the back of a spoon.

5 Bake for 15 minutes, or until lightly browned. Let cool in the pan for 10 minutes, then transfer the bites to a plate to cool completely. Repeat with any remaining quinoa mixture.

Makes 32 bites

Nonstick cooking spray

1 cup uncooked quinoa, rinsed if necessary (check the package directions)

1 cup water

2 egg whites

One 10-ounce package frozen spinach, cooked, cooled, and drained well

¼ cup grated Asiago cheese

PB&J Variation: *Skip the spinach and Asiago. Instead, stir in 2 tablespoons natural creamy peanut butter and ¼ cup finely chopped raisins.*

∙∙∙

Get-Your-Greens Nutrition per serving (2 bites): 52 calories; 3g protein; 1g fat (0g sat. fat); 7g carbohydrates; 1g fiber; 0g sugars; 44mg sodium; 31mg calcium; 0.6mg iron; 67mg potassium; 1mg vitamin C; 1,292IU vitamin A

PB&J Nutrition per serving (2 bites): 61 calories; 3g protein; 2g fat (0g sat. fat); 9g carbohydrates; 1g fiber; 1g sugars; 16mg sodium; 7mg calcium; 0.6mg iron; 84mg potassium; 0 mg vitamin C; 1IU vitamin A

CHICKEN NUGGETS

1 pound boneless, skinless chicken breasts

1 russet potato, peeled and cut into small chunks

¼ cup water

½ teaspoon onion powder

½ teaspoon garlic powder

Freshly ground black pepper

Nonstick cooking spray

½ cup plain fine bread crumbs

Age It Up: *Add ¾ teaspoon kosher salt to the chicken in step 2.*

These nuggets are made for dipping. Ketchup seems like a natural choice, but since it's full of salt and added sugars, try the Creamy Tomato Sauce on page 166 instead. If you do want to offer ketchup, mix 1 tablespoon with 2 tablespoons plain full-fat Greek yogurt for a more baby-friendly dunk.

1 Place the chicken and potato chunks in the multi-cooker. Pour in the water. Lock the lid and set to cook on high pressure for 6 minutes. When cooking is complete, press "Cancel" and carefully quick-release the pressure. Transfer the chicken and potatoes to a food processor, leaving most of the liquid behind in the pot. Let cool slightly.

2 Add the onion powder, garlic powder, and a few grinds of pepper to the food processor and process until smooth. Transfer the mixture to a medium bowl.

3 Preheat the broiler. Line a baking sheet with aluminum foil and spray the foil with cooking spray. Place the bread crumbs in a shallow dish. Form about 1 tablespoon of the chicken mixture into a nugget shape. Dip the nugget into the bread crumbs to coat, then place it on the prepared baking sheet. Repeat with the rest of the chicken mixture.

4 Spray the nuggets well with cooking spray. Broil until lightly browned on top, 1 to 2 minutes, then flip and broil until lightly browned on the second side, 1 to 2 minutes more.

Makes about 20 nuggets

Nutrition per serving (2 nuggets): 83 calories; 11g protein; 1g fat (0g sat. fat); 6g carbohydrates; 0g fiber; 0g sugars; 42mg sodium; 11mg calcium; 0.5mg iron; 249mg potassium; 1mg vitamin C; 12IU vitamin A

SALMON-CAULIFLOWER SLIDERS 🖐️ ❄️

1 Yukon Gold potato, peeled, cut into cubes

¾ cup water

One 6-ounce skinless salmon fillet, any bones removed

1 large cauliflower floret (3½ to 4-inches wide; about ¼ small head)

1 large egg

1 tablespoon unsalted butter

Age It Up: *Add ½ teaspoon salt in step 4. Serve on slider buns with a swipe of mayo.*

These savory patties are an all-in-one meal. Be sure salmon and other fatty fish are a regular part of your baby's diet. Their omega-3s are crucial for developing brains.

1 Place the potato cubes and water in the multi-cooker. Lock the lid and set to cook on high pressure for 5 minutes. When cooking is complete, press "Cancel" and carefully quick-release the pressure.

2 Remove the lid. Place the salmon and cauliflower on the metal rack that came with the multi-cooker and carefully lower the rack into the pot over the potatoes. Lock the lid and set to cook on low pressure for 2 minutes. When cooking is complete, press "Cancel" and let the pressure naturally release for 5 minutes, then carefully quick-release any remaining pressure.

3 Transfer the salmon and cauliflower to a large bowl. Break them into chunks to help them cool faster. Drain the potatoes and add them to the bowl. Let the mixture cool for about 10 minutes (you can use this time to clean up!).

4 Whisk the egg in a small bowl and add it to the salmon mixture. Mash everything together. Form the mixture into 2-inch patties.

5 In a large nonstick skillet, melt the butter over medium-high heat. Add the patties and cook until lightly browned on the first side, 3 to 4 minutes, lowering the heat if the butter or patties are burning. Flip and cook until lightly browned on the second side, 2 to 3 minutes more. (You can also cook the sliders in the multi-cooker set to the Sauté setting, although you may need a little extra butter to prevent sticking.)

Makes 8 sliders

· ·

Nutrition per slider: 73 calories; 6g protein; 3g fat (1g sat. fat); 5g carbohydrates; 1g fiber; 0g sugars; 22mg sodium; 11mg calcium; 0.5mg iron; 235mg potassium; 7mg vitamin C; 87IU vitamin A

BROCCOLI PATTIES ✋ ❄️

Nonstick cooking spray (preferably olive oil)

2 medium russet potatoes (about 1¼ pounds), peeled and cut into 1-inch pieces

2 cups small broccoli florets (from 1 head broccoli)

½ cup water

¼ cup nutritional yeast

1 teaspoon onion powder

½ teaspoon garlic powder

1 egg white

Age It Up: *Add ½ teaspoon kosher salt to the potato mixture in step 3 and/or sprinkle the patties with flaky sea salt after baking.*

Forming these kid classics into circles is the simplest method. But you can also make fun shapes by spraying a cookie cutter with nonstick cooking spray and molding the potato mixture inside the cutter on a parchment paper–lined baking sheet. Carefully remove the cutter and repeat.

• •

1 Place the potatoes and broccoli in the multi-cooker. Pour in the water. Lock the lid and set to cook on high pressure for 3 minutes. When cooking is complete, press "Cancel" and carefully quick-release the pressure. Remove the lid and let the vegetables cool for 10 minutes.

2 Preheat the oven to 375°F. Line a baking sheet with parchment paper and spray with nonstick cooking spray.

3 Using a potato masher, mash the potatoes and broccoli, then add the nutritional yeast, onion powder, and garlic powder and stir to combine. Mix in the egg white.

4 Form the potato mixture into patties about 2 inches in diameter, placing them on the prepared baking sheet as you go. Bake the patties for 16 minutes, flipping them once halfway through the cooking time.

Makes 18 patties

• •

Nutrition per serving (1 patty): 23 calories; 2g protein; 0g fat (0g sat. fat); 5g carbohydrates; 1g fiber; 0g sugars; 7mg sodium; 8mg calcium; 0.4mg iron; 130mg potassium; 9mg vitamin C; 237IU vitamin A

WHOLE CHICKEN

1 cup water

One 3- to 3½-pound whole chicken, giblets removed

Do not expect to end up with a golden, crispy-skinned roast chicken when cooking it in a multi-cooker. This chicken isn't browned at all, and you'll want to remove the skin after it's cooked. But what this bird lacks in looks, it makes up for in flavor and tenderness, ideal for shredding and serving to a self-feeding baby, plain or with a sauce. Why not just cook chicken breasts (see page 57)? Cooking a whole chicken is more economical—plus, you get dark meat and white meat in one package. Dark meat has more flavor, more of the healthy fats that babies need, and plentiful iron, zinc, and selenium.

1 Pour the water into the multi-cooker. Place the metal rack that came with the multi-cooker in the pot. Place the chicken breast-side up on the rack. Lock the lid and set to cook on high pressure for 20 minutes. When cooking is complete, press "Cancel" and let the pressure release naturally for 10 minutes, then carefully quick-release any remaining pressure.

2 Transfer the chicken to a cutting board. Let rest for at least 10 minutes before carving or shredding.

Makes about 4 cups shredded chicken

SLOW COOK IT: Place the whole chicken, breast side up, and 1 cup water in a 5- or 6-quart slow cooker. Cover and cook on Low for 6 hours, or until an instant-read thermometer inserted into the thigh (without touching bone) reads at least 165°F.

Nutrition per serving (¼ cup): 63 calories; 8g protein; 3g fat (1g sat. fat); 0g carbohydrates; 0g fiber; 0g sugars; 26mg sodium; 7mg calcium; 0.4mg iron; 69mg potassium; 0mg vitamin C; 1IU vitamin A

3 ways with shredded or chopped chicken for baby

Coat with a little Creamy Tomato Sauce (page 166).

Sprinkle with ground cumin or smoked paprika.

Toss with any vegetable purée.

DIY WALNUT BUTTER

It's easy to pick up almond butter at the store, and cashew butter is more and more available. But walnut butter is trickier to find. Happily, making it at home is super-easy.

Spread 5 ounces shelled walnuts (about 1½ cups) on a rimmed baking sheet. Toast in a 350°F oven until lightly browned, about 5 minutes. Let cool completely. Process the walnuts in a food processor until broken down almost to a powder. Add 2 teaspoons olive oil and process until smooth and creamy. Makes about ¾ cup.

Age It Up: *Add a pinch of kosher salt and a drizzle of maple syrup while processing.*

PUMPKIN OATS ❄

The multi-cooker is genius at cooking whole grains like steel-cut oats. There's no watching and stirring, no adding water if the level gets low. Just add everything, set the appliance, and walk away. You'll come back to perfectly cooked grains that are hearty and delicious for the whole family. For chewier oats, reduce the cooking time to 10 minutes.

1 tablespoon olive oil

1 cup steel-cut oats

3 cups water

½ cup canned pumpkin purée

¼ cup DIY Walnut Butter (see opposite; optional)

• •

1 Set the multi-cooker to Sauté and pour in the olive oil. When the oil is hot, add the oats and toast, stirring, for 1 to 2 minutes.

2 Pour in the water and stir to combine. Lock the lid and set to cook on high pressure for 12 minutes. When cooking is complete, press "Cancel" and let the pressure release naturally for 10 minutes, then carefully quick-release the remaining pressure.

3 Remove the lid and stir for a minute or two; the oats will thicken as they cool. Stir in the pumpkin and the walnut butter (if using), making sure no clumps remain.

Makes about 3½ cups

• •

SLOW COOK IT: Skip the olive oil. Spray a slow cooker insert with nonstick cooking spray. Stir together 1 cup steel-cut oats and 4½ cups water in the slow cooker. Cover and cook on Low for 8 hours. Continue with Step 3 of the recipe.

• •

Nutrition per serving (¼ cup): 54 calories; 2g protein; 2g fat (0g sat. fat); 8g carbohydrates; 2g fiber; 1g sugars; 2mg sodium; 3mg calcium; 0.6mg iron; 1mg potassium; 0mg vitamin C; 1,071IU vitamin A

Nutrition Note: *A spoonful or two of walnut butter stirred into these Pumpkin Oats is not only delicious, it adds brain-boosting omega-3 fatty acids and anti-oxidants to the bowl. Plus, it's an effective way to expose your little one to tree nuts (see page 35 for more on preventing food allergies).*

BEEF WITH BARLEY ✋ ❄️
AND CARROTS

½ pound boneless beef chuck, trimmed of fat and cut into 1-inch pieces

1 large carrot, peeled and cut into ½-inch pieces

¼ cup uncooked barley

½ cup low-sodium beef broth

Age It Up: *Add ¾ teaspoon kosher salt before cooking.*

There are three great ways to serve this stew: purée or mash it for beginning eaters, shred the beef and let baby self-feed, or let older babies and toddlers dig in with a spoon.

Combine the beef, carrot, barley, and broth in the multi-cooker. Lock the lid and set to cook on high pressure for 30 minutes. When cooking is complete, press "Cancel" and carefully quick-release the pressure.

Makes 2 cups

SLOW COOK IT: Double the recipe, but use 1 cup low-sodium beef broth and 1 cup water. Cover and cook on Low for 6 to 8 hours, or until the beef is very tender.

Nutrition per serving (¼ cup): 77 calories; 6g protein; 3g fat (1g sat. fat); 6g carbohydrates; 1g fiber; 0g sugars; 56mg sodium; 9mg calcium; 0.8mg iron; 136mg potassium; 0mg vitamin C; 1,279IU vitamin A

PURPLE SWEET POTATO 🖐 ❄
PATTIES

1½ cups water

3 medium purple sweet potatoes (about 2 pounds), peeled and cut into 1-inch-thick half-moons

1 large egg, beaten

2 scallions, thinly sliced

Freshly ground black pepper

2 tablespoons olive oil, plus more if necessary

Age It Up: *Add ¾ teaspoon kosher salt to the potato mixture in step 3, and serve with Cholula-spiked sour cream. To make it a meal, increase the size of the patties to 3 inches in diameter and top each with a fried egg.*

Sure, you could use regular orange sweet potatoes here. Or even russet potatoes. But one of our jobs when feeding babies is to introduce them to as many flavors, aromas, and, yes, colors as possible. Plus, purple sweet potatoes are brimming with potassium and vitamin A, so they're a great choice if you can find them.

1 Pour the water into the multi-cooker. Place a metal steamer basket into the pot. Place the sweet potatoes in the basket. Lock the lid and set to cook on high pressure for 4 minutes. When cooking is complete, press "Cancel" and carefully quick-release the pressure.

2 Transfer the potatoes to a large bowl. Let cool for 10 minutes.

3 Using a potato masher, mash the potatoes. Stir in the egg, scallions, and several twists of pepper. Form the potato mixture into 2-inch patties, placing them on a parchment-lined baking sheet as you go. You should have about 15 patties.

4 In a large nonstick or cast-iron skillet, heat 1 tablespoon of the olive oil over medium-high heat. Add as many patties as can comfortably fit in the pan with a little space between each and cook until golden brown on both sides, about 4 minutes total. Repeat with the remaining oil to cook the remaining patties.

Makes 15 patties

Nutrition per patty: 93 calories; 2g protein; 2g fat (0g sat. fat); 16g carbohydrates; 2g fiber; 2g sugars; 39mg sodium; 26mg calcium; 0.7mg iron; 214mg potassium; 7mg vitamin C; 93IU vitamin A

CHAPTER FOUR

- ALL -
TOGETHER
NOW
····(8 months and up)····

If you're looking for the secret sauce when it comes to raising an eager eater, look no further than the mirror. (Some parents might say the secret sauce is ketchup, but that's another story.) You—plus the other big kids or adults in your home—are the superstar of your baby's world, and he can't take his eyes off you. He is watching you and learning from you all the time, and nowhere more than at the table. That's why eating together—the same food at the same time—as often as possible is so powerful.

Everyday Recipes

The recipes in this chapter are meant for every member of the family. They are dishes that could be found in any other multi-cooker cookbook, except they are all perfect for baby: not too spicy, not too salty, and just the right texture for beginning eaters. Serve the dishes as written for bigger kids and grown-ups. For your baby, make sure the food is chopped or shredded into small pieces for self-feeding with fingers or a spoon. If your baby isn't ready for more advanced textures, most of these recipes can be either mashed or puréed for spoon-feeding.

Serve It Up

You'll notice that the serving sizes in this chapter are dramatically larger than in the previous chapters. The serving sizes here are geared toward the whole family, so don't expect that your little one will eat anywhere close to that amount. This means more for everyone else!

Well Seasoned

The recipes here include salt as an optional ingredient. If your child is under 12 months and actively partaking in these meals, skip the salt and add it at the table for big kids and grown-ups. Once your baby is a year old, you can start adding some salt to the recipes.

SAVORY OATS ✋

4 hard-boiled eggs (see page 60), unpeeled

2 tablespoons canola oil

8 ounces shiitake mushrooms, stemmed and thinly sliced

6 cups baby spinach (from one 5-ounce package)

½ teaspoon kosher salt (optional)

1 cup steel-cut oats

3 cups low-sodium vegetable broth

SLOW COOK IT: Spray a slow cooker insert with nonstick cooking spray. Combine 1 cup steel-cut oats, 4 cups low-sodium vegetable broth, and 1 cup water in a slow cooker. Cover and cook on Low for 8 hours. When the time is almost up, warm the eggs and cook the mushrooms and spinach on the stovetop as directed in steps 1 and 2. Serve the oats, vegetables, and eggs as described in step 5.

If you think of oats as a whole grain like farro or even brown rice, it makes sense to leave out the sweetener and top them with veggies. Babies can eat this meal with a spoon or just pick up the eggs and veggies (and even handfuls of oats!).

1 Remove the eggs from the fridge and place them in a bowl of warm water. (This will take the chill off the eggs.)

2 Set the multi-cooker to Sauté and pour in 1 tablespoon of the canola oil. When the oil is hot, add the mushrooms and cook until softened, about 5 minutes. Add the spinach and ¼ teaspoon of the salt (if using). Cook until the spinach is just wilted, about 1 minute. Transfer the mushroom mixture to a bowl.

3 Heat the remaining 1 tablespoon canola oil in the pot. When the oil is hot, add the oats and toast, stirring frequently, for 2 minutes. Add the broth and remaining ¼ teaspoon salt (if using). Lock the lid and set to cook on high pressure for 10 minutes. When cooking is complete, press "Cancel" and let the pressure release naturally for 10 minutes, then carefully quick-release any remaining pressure.

4 Meanwhile, drain the eggs, then peel and halve or chop them.

5 Stir the cooked oats for a minute or two; they will thicken. Serve the oats topped with the mushroom-spinach mixture and the eggs.

Makes 4 servings

Nutrition per serving: 342 calories; 15g protein; 15g fat (3g sat. fat); 37g carbohydrates; 8g fiber; 5g sugars; 237mg sodium; 121mg calcium; 5.9mg iron; 235mg potassium; 25mg vitamin C; 5,760IU vitamin A

SPICED PORK ✋ ❄️
WITH ORANGE CREMA

1 navel orange

⅓ cup sour cream

1 tablespoon ground cumin

2 teaspoons chili powder

2 teaspoons kosher salt (optional)

⅛ teaspoon ground cinnamon

One 2½- to 3-pound boneless pork shoulder roast, cut into 4 pieces

1 tablespoon olive oil

For the slaw

4 cups shredded cabbage

2 tablespoons olive oil

1 tablespoon apple cider vinegar

½ teaspoon kosher salt

¼ teaspoon sugar

The spice rub on this lusciously tender pork isn't *picante* spicy, so it's perfect for the whole family, including little ones. Serve it on buns, in tortillas, or on top of polenta. Save the crunchy slaw for the grown-ups and big kids at the table.

· ·

1 Zest the orange. In a small bowl, stir together the zest and the sour cream. Cover and refrigerate until ready to serve.

2 Halve the zested orange and squeeze the juice into a liquid measuring cup. Add water to the measuring cup to make ¾ cup liquid.

3 In a small bowl, stir together the cumin, chili powder, salt (if using), and cinnamon. Rub the spice mixture all over the pork pieces.

4 Set the multi-cooker to Sauté and pour in the olive oil. When the oil is hot, add 2 pieces of the pork and cook until well-browned, about 4 minutes per side. Transfer to a plate and repeat with the remaining pork pieces. Return all the pork to the cooker. Add the orange juice mixture. Lock the lid and set to cook on high pressure for 1 hour.

5 Meanwhile, make the slaw: In a medium bowl, combine all the slaw ingredients. Cover and refrigerate until ready to serve.

6 When cooking is complete, press "Cancel" and let the pressure release naturally for 15 minutes, then carefully quick-release any remaining pressure. Use a slotted spoon to transfer the pork to a cutting board; reserve the juices in the cooker. Shred the meat with two forks and transfer it to a serving platter or bowl. Spoon some of the juices from the cooker over the pork. Serve with the slaw and orange crema alongside.

Makes 6 servings

SLOW COOK IT: Complete steps 1 to 3 as directed above. Brown the pork in batches on the stovetop in olive oil in a large skillet. Transfer the pork to a 5- or 6-quart slow cooker. Pour over the orange juice mixture and add 1¼ cups water. Cover and cook on Low for 6 hours, or until the pork is tender. Make the slaw and shred and serve the pork as directed.

Nutrition per serving (including slaw): 445 calories; 46g protein; 26g fat (8g sat. fat); 6g carbohydrates; 2g fiber; 4g sugars; 368mg sodium; 76mg calcium; 3mg iron; 916mg potassium; 31mg vitamin C; 77IU vitamin A

BLACK BEAN AND SWEET POTATO STEW ✋ ❄

2 tablespoons olive oil

1 cup chopped onion

½ red or orange bell pepper, finely chopped

1 teaspoon ground cumin

1 teaspoon dried oregano

1 pound dried black beans, rinsed

5 cups water

2 teaspoons kosher salt (optional)

2 medium sweet potatoes (about 1 pound), cut into ½-inch cubes

1 cup canned diced tomatoes, with their juices

1 cup finely chopped fresh cilantro (optional)

Purée this stew for baby, or mash it slightly and serve it with a spoon or as a (messy!) finger food. Garnish with chopped avocado, a dollop of sour cream, and, for bigger eaters, crushed tortilla chips.

1 Set the multi-cooker to Sauté and pour in the olive oil. When the oil is hot, add the onion and bell pepper. Cook until tender, about 5 minutes. Add the cumin and oregano and cook, stirring, for 1 minute.

2 Add the beans, water, and salt (if using). Lock the lid and set to cook on high pressure for 35 minutes.

3 When cooking is completed, press "Cancel" and carefully quick-release the pressure. Stir in the sweet potatoes and tomatoes with their juices. Reseal the lid and set to cook on high pressure for 5 minutes more.

4 When cooking is completed, press "Cancel" and carefully quick-release the pressure. Stir in the cilantro (if using).

Makes 8 servings

Nutrition per serving: 285 calories; 14g protein; 4g fat (1g sat. fat); 50g carbohydrates; 11g fiber; 5g sugars; 102mg sodium; 101mg calcium; 3mg iron; 1,064mg potassium; 14mg vitamin C; 8,412IU vitamin A

SPRING LAMB SOUP ✋ ❄️

Shred or cut your baby's meat and chop the artichoke hearts into small pieces before serving.

. . . .

1 Sprinkle the lamb with 1¼ teaspoons of the salt (if using) and season with pepper. Set the multi-cooker to Sauté and pour in 1 tablespoon olive oil. When the oil is hot, add the lamb to the pot and cook, undisturbed, until browned on the bottom, 4 to 5 minutes. Flip and cook until browned on the second side, 4 to 5 minutes. Transfer the lamb to a plate.

2 Heat the remaining 1 teaspoon olive oil in the pot. Add the shallots, garlic, and remaining ¼ teaspoon salt (if using) and cook until the vegetables are softened, 2 to 3 minutes. Press "Cancel." Add the baby carrots, broth, and lamb, stirring to scrape up any browned bits on the bottom of the pot. Lock the lid and set to cook on high pressure for 20 minutes.

3 When cooking is complete, press "Cancel" and carefully quick-release the pressure. Remove the lid and set the multi-cooker to Sauté. Add the artichokes and peas to the pot and simmer to warm through, about 2 minutes. Stir in the lemon juice and dill.

Makes 4 servings

. . . .

SLOW COOK IT: Spray a slow cooker insert with nonstick cooking spray. Brown the lamb in a skillet in olive oil on the stovetop. Transfer the lamb to the slow cooker. Cook the shallots and garlic in the skillet until softened, about 2 minutes. Pour the shallot mixture over the lamb. Add the broth and carrots. Cover and cook on Low for 8 hours. Stir in the artichokes, peas, lemon juice, and dill.

. . . .

Nutrition per serving: 279 calories; 28g protein; 11g fat (3g sat. fat); 15g carbohydrates; 4g fiber; 5g sugars; 444mg sodium; 66mg calcium; 4.1mg iron; 456mg potassium; 10mg vitamin C; 4,678IU vitamin A

1 pound boneless lamb stew meat, trimmed of fat and cut into 1-inch pieces

1½ teaspoons kosher salt (optional)

Freshly ground black pepper

1 tablespoon plus 1 teaspoon olive oil

2 shallots, sliced

2 garlic cloves, thinly sliced

1 cup baby carrots

1¼ cups low-sodium chicken broth

One 14-ounce can whole artichoke hearts, drained and halved

½ cup frozen peas

2 teaspoons fresh lemon juice

1 tablespoon chopped fresh dill

CAULIFLOWER 30 MAC 'N' CHEESE

Feel free to just stir in ¾ cup cauliflower purée (see page 56) or even butternut squash purée (see page 53) if you already have it on hand rather than cooking the cauliflower with the pasta. If you're pulling the purée out of the freezer, thaw it before adding to the pasta.

8 ounces dried elbow macaroni

1¾ cups water

1½ teaspoons plus ⅛ teaspoon kosher salt (optional)

½ head cauliflower, cut into 2- to 3-inch florets (about 2½ cups)

2 teaspoons unsalted butter

¼ cup panko bread crumbs

½ teaspoon paprika

½ cup evaporated milk, plus more if necessary

1½ cups grated cheddar cheese

¾ teaspoon dried mustard

1 Stir together the macaroni, water, and 1½ teaspoons of the salt (if using) in the multi-cooker. Arrange the cauliflower on top. Lock the lid and set to cook on high pressure for 4 minutes.

2 Meanwhile, in a small skillet, melt the butter over medium-high heat. Add the panko, paprika, and remaining ⅛ teaspoon salt (if using) and cook, stirring, until the panko is toasted, 2 to 3 minutes. Remove from the heat and transfer to a bowl.

3 When cooking is complete, press "Cancel" and carefully quick-release the pressure. Transfer the cauliflower to a plate and cut into smaller florets.

4 Add the evaporated milk, cheese, and mustard to the pot with the pasta and stir until creamy. Add more evaporated milk, if necessary. Return the cauliflower to the pot and stir to coat. Serve sprinkled with the toasted panko.

Makes 4 servings

Nutrition per serving: 384 calories; 17g protein; 12g fat (7g sat. fat); 52g carbohydrates; 3g fiber; 6g sugars; 208mg sodium; 264mg calcium; 2.3mg iron; 436mg potassium; 35mg vitamin C; 287IU vitamin A

GREEK ✋ ❄
MEATBALL PITAS

1 large egg

1 pound 80% lean ground beef

1 small zucchini, grated and squeezed dry in clean kitchen towel (about 2 cups)

2 garlic cloves, grated

Zest of 1 lemon

1½ teaspoons dried oregano

¼ cup panko bread crumbs

1¼ teaspoons kosher salt (optional)

1 tablespoon olive oil

½ cup low-sodium chicken broth

½ cup plain full-fat Greek yogurt

4 pita pockets

2 plum tomatoes, chopped

4 romaine lettuce leaves, shredded

SLOW COOK IT: Spray a slow cooker insert with nonstick cooking spray. Pour in the broth. Place the meatballs in the slow cooker with the broth. Cover and cook on Low for 6 hours. Make the tzatziki and serve as directed above.

Deconstruct your baby's portion by cutting the meatballs and pita into small pieces for self-feeding. Serve with chopped tomato and the tzatziki for dipping.

1 Crack the egg into a large bowl and beat with a fork. Add the beef, half the zucchini, the garlic, lemon zest, oregano, panko, and 1 teaspoon of the salt (if using). Form the mixture into 12 meatballs.

2 Set the multi-cooker to Sauté and pour in the olive oil. When the oil is hot, add the meatballs and brown on one side, about 3 minutes. Carefully turn them over with tongs and brown on the second side, about 3 minutes (it's okay if a little meat sticks to the bottom of the pot). Press "Cancel." Pour in the broth. Lock the lid and set to cook on high pressure for 5 minutes. Press "Cancel" and let the pressure release naturally for 10 minutes, then carefully quick-release any remaining pressure.

3 While the meatballs are cooking, stir together the yogurt, remaining zucchini, remaining ¼ teaspoon salt (if using), and 1 tablespoon cold water. Refrigerate the tzatziki until ready to serve.

4 Serve the meatballs in pita pockets with the tzatziki, chopped tomato, and shredded lettuce.

Makes 4 servings

Nutrition per serving: 549 calories; 30g protein; 30g fat (10g sat. fat); 39g carbohydrates; 3g fiber; 5g sugars; 473mg sodium; 183mg calcium; 4.8mg iron; 537mg potassium; 12mg vitamin C; 678IU vitamin A

CHICKEN CURRY ❄ MEATBALLS

1 large egg

1 pound ground chicken (white and dark meat)

2 tablespoons dried bread crumbs

2 teaspoons curry powder

¾ teaspoon kosher salt (optional)

¼ cup finely chopped fresh chives, plus more for garnish

1 tablespoon coconut oil or canola oil

½ cup low-sodium chicken broth

1 tablespoon unsalted butter

SLOW COOK IT: Spray a slow cooker insert with nonstick cooking spray. Pour in the broth. Add the meatballs. Cover and cook on Low for 6 hours. In step 3, after removing the meatballs, transfer the liquid from the slow cooker to a saucepan and continue with the recipe.

It's almost like the multi-cooker was invented to cook meatballs for babies. These savory nuggets are so flavorful and tender—no dry meatballs here! Serve with store-bought naan or over rice, if you can handle cleaning up the mess.

1 Crack the egg into a large bowl and beat with a fork. Add the ground chicken, bread crumbs, curry powder, and salt (if using). Combine with a fork. Mix in the chives. Form the chicken mixture into 12 to 15 meatballs.

2 Set the multi-cooker to Sauté and heat the coconut oil in the pot. When the oil is hot, add the meatballs and brown on one side, about 3 minutes (no need to flip). Add the broth and press "Cancel." Lock the lid and set to cook on high pressure for 5 minutes. When cooking is complete, press "Cancel" and let the pressure release naturally for 10 minutes, then carefully quick-release any remaining pressure.

3 Transfer the meatballs to a serving dish, reserving the liquid in the cooker. Set the multi-cooker to Sauté and let the broth simmer for 3 minutes to reduce it slightly, scraping up any browned bits from the bottom of the pot with a wooden spoon. Press "Cancel" and stir in the butter. Serve the meatballs topped with the sauce and garnished with chives.

Makes 4 servings

Nutrition per serving: 252 calories; 22g protein; 17g fat (8g sat. fat); 3g carbohydrates; 1g fiber; 0g sugars; 119mg sodium; 29mg calcium; 1.6mg iron; 631mg potassium; 2mg vitamin C; 287IU vitamin A

CHEESY MUSHROOM ❄ 30 RISOTTO

1 cup dried porcini mushrooms

2 cups hot water

2 tablespoons olive oil

½ cup finely chopped shallots

1½ cups Arborio rice

½ cup apple cider

2 cups low-sodium chicken broth or vegetable broth

1 teaspoon kosher salt (optional)

4 ounces Gruyère cheese, grated (about 1 cup)

1 tablespoon unsalted butter

2 tablespoons chopped fresh chives

Multi-cookers are genius at cooking risotto—no standing at the stove stirring! It's so easy, it almost feels like cheating.

• •

1 Place the mushrooms in a small bowl and pour the hot water over them. Let soak for 15 minutes. Drain the mushrooms through a fine-mesh sieve set over a 2-cup measuring cup, taking care to leave any grit behind in the bowl. Add water to the mushroom soaking liquid to make 2 cups. Chop the mushrooms and set aside.

2 Set the multi-cooker to Sauté and pour in the olive oil. When the oil is hot, add the shallots and cook, stirring frequently, until tender, about 3 minutes. Add the rice and toast, stirring, until the edges of the grains are translucent, about 3 minutes. Pour in the apple cider and cook until most of the cider has been absorbed.

3 Add the mushrooms, reserved mushroom soaking water, broth, and salt (if using). Lock the lid and set to cook on high pressure for 6 minutes.

4 When cooking is complete, press "Cancel" and carefully quick-release the pressure. Stir in the cheese and butter. Continue to stir for 2 to 3 minutes, until the risotto has thickened. Serve topped with chives.

Makes 5 servings

. . . .

SLOW COOK IT: Soak, drain, and chop the mushrooms, reserving the soaking liquid, as described in step 1. Complete step 2 on the stovetop and then transfer the rice mixture to a slow cooker. Add the mushrooms, reserved mushroom soaking water, broth, and salt (if using). Cover and cook on High for 1 to 2 hours, until the rice is just tender. Finish and serve the risotto as directed in step 4.

. . . .

Nutrition per serving: 452 calories; 16g protein; 16g fat (6g sat. fat); 61g carbohydrates; 3g fiber; 4g sugars; 199mg sodium; 240mg calcium; 1.6mg iron; 96mg potassium; 8mg vitamin C; 339IU vitamin A

LEMONY RISOTTO

This is the perfect meal for your baby to practice her spoon skills, since the risotto is thick enough that at least some of it will make it from the bowl to her mouth. Save leftovers for the Arancini on page 160.

2 tablespoons olive oil

1 cup finely chopped onion

1½ cups Arborio rice

4 cups low-sodium chicken broth

¾ teaspoon kosher salt (optional)

½ cup grated Parmesan cheese

1 tablespoon unsalted butter

Zest of 1 lemon

1 to 2 tablespoons fresh lemon juice

Freshly ground black pepper

1 Set the multi-cooker to Sauté and pour in the olive oil. When the oil is hot, add the onion and cook, stirring frequently, until tender, about 3 minutes. Add the rice and toast, stirring, until the edges of the grains are translucent, about 3 minutes. Stir in the broth and salt (if using). Lock the lid and set to cook on high pressure for 6 minutes.

2 When cooking is complete, press "Cancel" and carefully quick-release the pressure. Stir in the cheese and butter. Continue to stir for 2 to 3 minutes, until the risotto has thickened. Add the lemon zest and lemon juice, plus plenty of pepper, and serve.

Makes 5 servings (about 5½ cups)

SLOW COOK IT: Complete step 1 on the stovetop through the toasting of the rice. Add ¼ cup of the broth and stir to scrape up any browned bits from the bottom of the pan. Transfer the rice mixture to a slow cooker. Add the remaining 3¾ cups broth and the salt (if using). Cover and cook on High for 1 to 2 hours. Finish and serve the risotto as directed in step 2.

Nutrition per serving: 468 calories; 16g protein; 15g fat (5g sat. fat); 71g carbohydrates; 2g fiber; 2g sugars; 263mg sodium; 151mg calcium; 0.6mg iron; 86mg potassium; 8mg vitamin C; 199IU vitamin A

ARANCINI ✋ ❄

1 cup panko bread crumbs

1 large egg

2½ cups cold risotto

½ cup butternut squash purée (see page 53)

¼ teaspoon kosher salt (optional)

¼ cup all-purpose flour

1 ounce fontina cheese, cut into 12 cubes

Nonstick cooking spray (preferably olive oil)

Creamy Tomato Sauce (page 166) or store-bought marinara sauce, for serving (optional)

It is so simple to make risotto in the multi-cooker that it's no hardship to cook a batch just for making these savory little nuggets. You can also use leftover Lemony Risotto (page 159). Make sure the risotto has spent at least six hours, and up to two days, chilling in the fridge.

● ●

1 Preheat the oven to 375°F. Spread the panko in a thin layer on a rimmed baking sheet and toast in the oven until golden, 5 to 7 minutes, stirring once. Transfer the panko to a shallow dish and line the same baking sheet with parchment paper.

2 Crack the egg into a large bowl and beat it with a fork. Add the risotto, butternut squash purée, and salt (if using). Form the risotto mixture into 12 balls, placing them on the prepared baking sheet as you go. The mixture will seem wet, and the balls won't perfectly hold their shape yet, but don't worry.

3 Place the flour in a separate shallow dish and set it next to the dish. Flatten a risotto ball into a disc. Place a cube of fontina in the middle and re-form the risotto mixture into a ball around the cheese. Roll the ball first in the flour, then in the panko, and return it to the baking sheet. Repeat to fill and coat the remaining risotto balls. Spray each ball with cooking spray.

4 Bake the risotto balls for 15 minutes. Remove the pan from the oven, turn each ball with tongs, and spray again with cooking spray. Bake for 15 minutes more. Serve with tomato sauce or marinara for dipping.

Makes 4 servings

● ●

Nutrition per serving: 357 calories; 14g protein; 10g fat (4g sat. fat); 54g carbohydrates; 3g fiber; 2g sugars; 219mg sodium; 141mg calcium; 1.3mg iron; 262mg potassium; 15mg vitamin C; 6,008IU vitamin A

MEXICAN-STYLE ✋ ❄ ⑳ MASH BOWLS

1¼ pounds Yukon Gold or russet potatoes, peeled and cut into 1-inch chunks

4 cups large cauliflower florets (12 ounces, from 1 head cauliflower)

½ cup water

¼ cup whole milk

2 tablespoons unsalted butter

½ teaspoon kosher salt (optional)

Toppings

4 slices bacon

1 cup cooked or canned black beans (see page 47), drained and rinsed if canned

¼ cup mild salsa

3 scallions, thinly sliced

1 cup grated cheddar cheese

Hot sauce or more salsa (optional)

A choose-your-own-adventure dinner in more ways than one, with a creamy mash—your choice of cauliflower-potato, just potato, or sweet potato—plus toppings for family members to build their own bowls.

1 Combine the potatoes, cauliflower, and water in the multi-cooker. Lock the lid and set to cook on high pressure for 5 minutes.

2 Meanwhile, in a microwave-safe measuring cup, gently heat the milk and butter together in the microwave until the butter has melted.

3 Prep the toppings: Cook the bacon on the stovetop or in the oven until crisp. Chop it into small pieces and place them in a small bowl. Combine the beans and salsa and warm in the microwave or on the stovetop. Place the scallions and cheese in separate small bowls.

4 When the potatoes and cauliflower have finished cooking, press "Cancel" and carefully quick-release the pressure. Pour the warmed milk-butter mixture into the pot. Add the salt (if using). Mash everything with a potato masher until smooth. Serve with the prepared toppings and hot sauce or more salsa, if desired.

Makes 4 servings

Nutrition per serving: 395 calories; 17g protein; 19g fat (10g sat. fat); 43g carbohydrates; 9g fiber; 5g sugars; 397mg sodium; 282mg calcium; 3mg iron; 1,097mg potassium; 71mg vitamin C; 694IU vitamin A

Potato or Sweet Potato Variation: *Cook 2 pounds chopped peeled Yukon Gold potatoes or sweet potatoes as directed in step 1. Increase the butter to 3 tablespoons and the salt to ¾ teaspoon (if using). This makes 4 cups of potatoes, so you'll probably have some leftovers.*

LENTIL ✋ ❄️
BOLOGNESE

1 tablespoon olive oil

1 cup chopped onion

2 garlic cloves, thinly sliced

1 carrot, diced

1 celery stalk, diced

8 ounces mushrooms, quartered

1¼ teaspoons kosher salt (optional)

2 teaspoons dried Italian seasoning

1 tablespoon tomato paste

1 cup French lentils (a.k.a. de Puy lentils), rinsed

1½ cups marinara sauce

1½ cups low-sodium chicken broth or vegetable broth

10 ounces rigatoni pasta

1 tablespoon red wine vinegar

Grated Parmesan cheese, for serving (optional)

Ingredient Tip! *It's easy to make your own marinara sauce, but if you're buying a jar at the store, look for one with no added sugar.*

If any food deserves to be labeled a "superfood," it's lentils. Packed with folate, fiber, protein, and iron, they are a stellar addition to your whole family's diet, and especially to your baby's.

1 Set the multi-cooker to Sauté and pour in the olive oil. When the oil is hot, add the onion, garlic, carrot, celery, mushrooms, salt (if using), and Italian seasoning. Cook until the vegetables are soft, 5 to 6 minutes. Add the tomato paste and stir to coat the vegetables, about 30 seconds. Press "Cancel."

2 Add the lentils, marinara sauce, and broth. Lock the lid and set to cook on high pressure for 28 minutes.

3 Meanwhile, cook the rigatoni according to the package directions and drain.

4 When cooking is complete, press "Cancel" and carefully quick-release the pressure.

5 Stir in the pasta and vinegar. Serve topped with Parmesan, if desired.

Makes 6 servings

Nutrition per serving: 415 calories; 20g protein; 6g fat (0g sat. fat); 72g carbohydrates; 15g fiber; 13g sugars; 420mg sodium; 70mg calcium; 6.2mg iron; 629mg potassium; 7mg vitamin C; 3,164IU vitamin A

GINGERED ✋ ❄ ③⓪ MEAT & POTATOES

This recipe is a multi-cooker–ready and baby-friendly take on one of my favorite recipes from the terrific cookbook *Keepers* by Caroline Campion and Kathy Brennan. It's a quick-cooking mix of ground meat, carrots, and potatoes seasoned with ginger and a little brown sugar. A keeper indeed.

1 tablespoon canola oil

1 pound lean ground beef

½ cup chopped onion

½ teaspoon kosher salt (optional)

1 teaspoon grated fresh ginger

¾ cup low-sodium chicken broth

1 teaspoon dark brown sugar

2 carrots, cut on an angle into ½-inch-thick slices

2 russet potatoes, peeled and cut into 1-inch chunks

2 cups baby spinach

3 scallions, sliced

Soy sauce and Sriracha, for serving (optional)

1 Set the multi-cooker to Sauté and pour in the canola oil. When the oil is hot, add the ground beef, onion, and ¼ teaspoon salt (if using) and cook, breaking up the beef with a wooden spoon, until the meat is no longer pink, about 5 minutes. Add the ginger and cook for 1 minute more. Press "Cancel." Using a slotted spoon, transfer the beef mixture to a bowl. Carefully pour out any fat in the pot and wipe out the pot with a paper towel. Return the pot to the multi-cooker.

2 Combine the broth and brown sugar in the pot and stir to scrape up any browned bits from the bottom of the pot. Stir in the carrots, potatoes, and remaining ¼ teaspoon salt (if using). Lock the lid and set to cook on high pressure for 4 minutes.

3 When cooking is complete, press "Cancel" and carefully quick-release the pressure. Stir in the baby spinach and cooked beef. Serve topped with scallions and, for the non-babies at the table, drizzled with soy sauce and Sriracha.

Makes 4 servings

Nutrition per serving: 305 calories; 28g protein; 9g fat (3g sat. fat); 27g carbohydrates; 4g fiber; 4g sugars; 139mg sodium; 74mg calcium; 4.9mg iron; 997mg potassium; 19mg vitamin C; 7,042IU vitamin A

CREAMY ❄ TOMATO SAUCE

2 tablespoons olive oil

1 small onion, chopped

1 carrot, finely chopped

1 tablespoon tomato paste

One 28-ounce can whole tomatoes, crushed or coarsely chopped (see Note)

¾ teaspoon kosher salt (optional)

2 tablespoons heavy cream

This versatile sauce is delicious on pasta, of course, or as a topping for breaded chicken cutlets or a dip for cheesy toast.

1   Set the multi-cooker to Sauté and pour in the olive oil. When the oil is hot, add the onion and carrot and cook, stirring frequently, until very tender, about 10 minutes. If the pot gets too hot and the vegetables start to brown, add a little water. Add the tomato paste and cook, stirring, for 1 minute.

2   Add the tomatoes with their juices and the salt (if using). Lock the lid and set to cook on high pressure for 6 minutes.

3   When cooking is complete, press "Cancel" and carefully quick-release the pressure. Remove the lid and cool slightly. Using an immersion blender, or in an upright blender, blend until smooth. Stir in the cream.

Makes 3 cups

SLOW COOK IT: Double the recipe. Omit the olive oil and instead combine the onion, carrot, tomato paste, tomatoes, and salt (if using) in a slow cooker. Cover and cook on Low for 6 hours. Blend the sauce until smooth and then stir in the cream.

Nutrition per serving (½ cup): 94 calories; 1g protein; 6g fat (2g sat. fat); 9g carbohydrates; 3g fiber; 6g sugars; 279mg sodium; 27mg calcium; 0.5mg iron; 50mg potassium; 11mg vitamin C; 2,307IU vitamin A

a trick for canned tomatoes

You can crush a can of whole tomatoes by emptying everything into a bowl and squeezing the tomatoes with your clean hands. Or my favorite method, because it dirties one less bowl, is to open the can, remove the lid, and use kitchen shears to snip the tomatoes right inside the can. This strategy works especially well in this recipe, since the sauce is blended up at the end.

cheers!

RECOMMENDED DRINKS FOR BABIES

Before age one, a baby's primary source of hydration is breastmilk or formula. But learning how to drink from a cup is part of the feeding process.

According to the American Academy of Pediatrics (AAP), once your child is six months old, he can start drinking from a cup. It seems intuitive to start with a sippy cup to make drinking easy and to minimize spills. However, some experts feel that the sippy cup should be skipped altogether, since it can impede oral-motor development. If you choose to give your baby a sippy cup, don't allow it in his crib at night, and be sure to transition him to an open cup by one year of age.

If you want to skip the sippy cup, start with an open cup. The idea of handing your baby an open cup and expecting him to actually drink out of it may make you laugh out loud. But start with just a little water in the cup, and you'll be surprised at how quickly your baby gets the hang of it. By 12 months, he will likely be able to maneuver the cup with his hands.

Another option is a cup with a straw, which most babies can handle at around eight to ten months.

At one year, your baby should be drinking from an open cup. You'll want to phase out the bottle altogether between 12 and 24 months.

So what's the best drink for babies, aside from breastmilk and formula? Good old water. Once your baby turns six months of age, or when you feel he is ready, place an open cup or sippy cup of water on his high-chair tray whenever he is eating. Between six and 12 months of age, you can offer your child four to six ounces of water per day.

Cow's milk or fortified soy milk should not be introduced until one year, as your baby's body cannot digest them properly. Plus, these are likely to fill him up so much that he'll reject breastmilk, formula, or solids. It's okay to use a little cow's milk in cooking or baking and to serve other dairy foods such as yogurt or cheese.

Juice should be avoided until your baby is a toddler. (Even then, the AAP recommends that toddlers limit consumption to no more than four to six ounces per day.) In addition, all sugar-sweetened beverages—including sweet tea, sports drinks, lemonades, juice drinks, and soda—should be avoided completely.

SPLIT PEA AND SAUSAGE SOUP

Preload your baby's spoon for this protein-rich meal, or let her pick out the small pieces of sausage as a finger food. Toast sticks would make for a great dipper.

. . . .

1 Set the multi-cooker to Sauté and pour in 1 tablespoon of the olive oil. When the oil is hot, add the sausage to the pot. Cook, stirring frequently, until browned and cooked through, about 5 minutes. Use a slotted spoon to transfer the sausage to a bowl.

2 Heat the remaining 1 tablespoon olive oil in the pot. Add the fennel and celery and cook until tender and caramelized, about 10 minutes, adding a little water if the vegetables seem to be browning too quickly. Add the garlic and cook for 1 minute more.

3 Add the split peas, broth, and salt (if using). Lock the lid and set to cook on high pressure for 15 minutes.

4 When cooking is complete, press "Cancel" and carefully quick-release the pressure. Stir frequently for a couple of minutes; the soup should thicken somewhat. Stir in the cooked sausage, spinach, vinegar, and pepper.

Makes 6 servings

. . . .

Nutrition per serving: 392 calories; 25g protein; 17g fat (5g sat. fat); 37g carbohydrates; 15g fiber; 5g sugars; 618mg sodium; 97mg calcium; 4mg iron; 856mg potassium; 12mg vitamin C; 3,515IU vitamin A

2 tablespoons olive oil

8 ounces mild Italian sausage, casings removed if necessary

1 cup finely chopped fennel (about ½ bulb) or onion

1 celery stalk, finely chopped

2 garlic cloves, chopped

1½ cups dried split peas, rinsed

6 cups low-sodium chicken broth

1 teaspoon kosher salt (optional)

One 10-ounce package frozen spinach, defrosted and drained well

2 teaspoons white wine vinegar

Freshly ground black pepper

SHAKSHUKA 30

1 tablespoon olive oil

1 small onion, chopped

2 garlic cloves, sliced

2 teaspoons smoked paprika

1 teaspoon ground cumin

1 teaspoon kosher salt (optional)

One 12-ounce jar roasted red peppers, drained and chopped

One 28-ounce can fire-roasted crushed tomatoes

One 15-ounce can low-sodium chickpeas, drained and rinsed

4 large eggs

Chopped fresh cilantro, for garnish

⅓ cup crumbled feta cheese (optional)

Pita bread, for serving (optional)

To play it safe on the food-safety front, it's best to skip runny egg yolks for babies. (Sorry, babies.) The yolks in this dish are fully cooked, almost like a hard-boiled egg. You will likely have leftovers of this hearty, smoky sauce. Save it for eating on toast or as a stew for lunch.

1 Set the multi-cooker to Sauté and pour in the olive oil. When the oil is hot, add the onion and garlic and cook until slightly softened, about 3 minutes. Stir in the paprika, cumin, and salt (if using) and cook for 1 minute more. Press "Cancel."

2 Stir in the roasted red peppers and tomatoes. Lock the lid and set to cook on high pressure for 5 minutes.

3 When cooking is complete, press "Cancel" and carefully quick-release the pressure. Stir in the chickpeas. Working with one egg at a time, crack an egg into a ramekin and tip the egg into the sauce. Repeat with the remaining eggs. Lock the lid and set to cook on low pressure for 2 minutes.

4 When cooking is complete, press "Cancel" and carefully quick-release the pressure. Serve sprinkled with cilantro and feta (if using), and with pita bread, if desired.

Makes 4 servings

Nutrition per serving: 321 calories; 14g protein; 9g fat (2g sat. fat); 41g carbohydrates; 9g fiber; 11g sugars; 653mg sodium; 141mg calcium; 4.8mg iron; 112mg potassium; 25mg vitamin C; 3,659IU vitamin A

BUTTERNUT SQUASH AND KALE FARROTTO ✋ ❄️

Save prep time by using precut butternut squash and pre-washed baby kale. If you do buy prewashed kale or any other greens, there's no need to rewash them at home. They're actually cleaned very well, and you have a greater chance of recontaminating them in your own kitchen!

1 tablespoon olive oil

1 small onion, chopped

4 cups curly kale leaves (about 4 ounces), finely chopped

2 teaspoons kosher salt (optional)

1½ cups uncooked farro

5 cups chopped (1-inch pieces) peeled butternut squash (from 1 medium squash)

2½ cups low-sodium chicken broth

1 tablespoon unsalted butter

Zest of 1 lemon

Grated Parmesan cheese, for serving (optional)

1 Set the multi-cooker to Sauté and pour in the olive oil. When the oil is hot, add the onion, kale, and 1 teaspoon of the salt (if using) and cook until the kale is tender and wilted, about 4 minutes. Add the farro and cook until toasted, about 1 minute. Press "Cancel." Stir in the squash and broth. Lock the lid and set to cook on high pressure for 10 minutes.

2 When cooking is complete, press "Cancel" and let the pressure naturally release for 10 minutes, then carefully quick-release any remaining pressure.

3 Stir in the butter, lemon zest, and remaining 1 teaspoon salt (if using). Serve with grated Parmesan, if desired.

Makes 6 servings

SLOW COOK IT: Omit the olive oil and onion. Combine the farro, 4 cups broth, and 1 teaspoon of the salt (if using) in a slow cooker. Add the kale and squash. Cover and cook on High for 3 to 4 hours, or until the farro and squash are tender, stirring once after 2 hours. Continue with Step 3.

Nutrition per serving: 317 calories; 10g protein; 6g fat (2g sat. fat); 56g carbohydrates; 10g fiber; 3g sugars; 66mg sodium; 172mg calcium; 4.2mg iron; 631mg potassium; 85mg vitamin C; 13,846IU vitamin A

CHICKEN AND VEG STEW

2 tablespoons olive oil

1 small onion, chopped

2 garlic cloves, sliced

½ teaspoon grated fresh ginger

2 boneless, skinless chicken breasts (about 1¼ pounds total)

2 cups low-sodium chicken broth

½ teaspoon kosher salt (optional)

1 medium zucchini, cut into ½-inch cubes

8 ounces asparagus, cut into ½-inch-long pieces, tips left whole

1 cup frozen peas

Serve your baby's portion of this springy meal without the broth as a finger food. Don't be surprised if he simply picks out his favorite bits and leaves the rest. That's 100% okay!

1 Set the multi-cooker to Sauté and pour in the olive oil. When the oil is hot, add the onion and cook, stirring frequently, until tender, about 5 minutes. Add the garlic and ginger and cook for 1 minute more.

2 Add the chicken breasts, broth, and salt (if using). Lock the lid and set to cook on high pressure for 10 minutes.

3 When cooking is complete, press "Cancel" and carefully quick-release the pressure. Transfer the chicken to a plate to cool.

4 Add the zucchini and asparagus to the pot, lock the lid, and set to cook on high pressure for 1 minute. When cooking is complete, press "Cancel" and carefully quick-release the pressure. Stir in the peas.

5 When the chicken is cool enough to handle, shred the meat and stir it into the stew.

Makes 4 servings

Nutrition per serving: 294 calories; 38g protein; 11g fat (2g sat. fat); 11g carbohydrates; 3g fiber; 4g sugars; 383mg sodium; 45mg calcium; 3mg iron; 851mg potassium; 16mg vitamin C; 713IU vitamin A

SLOW COOK IT: Spray a slow cooker insert with nonstick cooking spray. Sauté the onion in olive oil in a skillet on the stovetop for about 5 minutes; add the garlic and ginger and cook another minute. Transfer the mixture to the slow cooker. Add the chicken, broth, and salt (if using). Cover and cook on Low for 6 hours. Stir in the zucchini, asparagus, and peas, cover, and cook for 30 minutes to 1 hour more, until the vegetables are tender and the chicken is cooked through.

CLASSIC  POT ROAST

1 tablespoon olive oil

One 3-pound boneless chuck roast

2 teaspoons kosher salt (optional)

2 tablespoons tomato paste

½ cup low-sodium beef broth

½ pound baby carrots

6 ounces frozen pearl onions (1½ cups)

¼ cup pitted green olives, halved

Chopped fresh flat-leaf parsley, for garnish

Your entire family—baby included—will devour this tender meat; just cut your baby's portion into smaller bites. Serve over polenta or mashed potatoes.

1 Set the multi-cooker to Sauté and pour in the olive oil. Sprinkle the roast with the salt (if using). Place the roast in the pot and brown on one side for 5 to 6 minutes. Flip and brown on the second side, 5 to 6 minutes more. Transfer the roast to a plate. Press "Cancel."

2 Add the tomato paste and broth to the pot and stir to combine, scraping up any browned bits from the bottom of the pot. Return the roast to the pot. Lock the lid and set to cook on high pressure for 1 hour.

3 When cooking is complete, press "Cancel" and carefully quick-release the pressure. Transfer the meat to a cutting board; tent it loosely with aluminum foil and let rest. Discard all but 1 cup of the cooking liquid. Add the carrots and onions to the pot. Lock the lid and set to cook on high pressure for 4 minutes. When cooking is complete, press "Cancel" and carefully quick-release the pressure.

4 Slice the meat, removing any excess fat or gristle, and place on a serving platter. Use a spoon to transfer the vegetables and some juices to the platter, arranging them around and over the meat. Garnish with the olives and parsley.

Makes 6 servings

Nutrition per serving: 366 calories; 48g protein; 17g fat (7g sat. fat); 7g carbohydrates; 2g fiber; 4g sugars; 290mg sodium; 60mg calcium; 5.6mg iron; 900mg potassium; 4mg vitamin C; 5,282IU vitamin A

SALSA  CHICKEN

Skip the tortilla chips in your baby's portion of this saucy chicken. Even though they're soft, the chips might be too challenging to chew. This means more for you. (You're welcome.)

8 ounces crème fraîche (such as Vermont Creamery brand)

1 cup mild tomato salsa

¼ teaspoon kosher salt (optional)

1 pound thinly sliced chicken cutlets (about 4)

2 cups tortilla chips (about 2 ounces)

Chopped fresh cilantro, for garnish (optional)

1 Stir together the crème fraiche, salsa, and salt (if using) in the multi-cooker. Add the chicken and turn to coat. Lock the lid and set to cook on high pressure for 3 minutes.

2 When cooking is complete, press "Cancel" and let the pressure release naturally; this will take about 5 minutes.

3 Transfer the chicken to a plate. Break the tortilla chips into pieces with your hands and drop them into the sauce in the multi-cooker. Stir to coat and let sit for 5 minutes.

4 Serve the chicken covered with sauce and softened chips, and topped with cilantro, if desired.

Makes 4 servings, plus extra sauce

Nutrition per serving: 255 calories; 26g protein; 14g fat (8g sat. fat); 3g carbohydrates; 1g fiber; 2g sugars; 284mg sodium; 75mg calcium; 0.6mg iron; 471mg potassium; 1mg vitamin C; 684IU vitamin A

THAI ✋ 🕥
SHRIMP CURRY

1 cup unsweetened canned coconut milk, stirred

1 teaspoon Thai red curry paste, plus more to taste

¾ teaspoon kosher salt (optional)

1 red bell pepper, cut into 1-inch pieces

1½ cups 1-inch butternut squash cubes

1 pound large shrimp, peeled and deveined

1 teaspoon fish sauce (optional)

Chopped fresh cilantro and/or Thai basil, for garnish

Lime wedges, for serving

Introduce your baby to Southeast Asian flavors with this mild and quick-cooking curry. Serve it over rice, with some Sriracha for adults and older kids who like extra heat.

. . . .

1 Whisk together the coconut milk, curry paste, and salt (if using) in the multi-cooker. Add the bell pepper, squash, and shrimp and stir to coat. Lock the lid and set to cook on high pressure for 2 minutes.

2 When cooking is complete, press "Cancel" and carefully quick-release the pressure.

3 Stir in the fish sauce (if using). Garnish with cilantro and/or Thai basil, and serve with lime wedges.

Makes 4 servings

. . . .

Nutrition per serving: 148 calories; 24g protein; 2g fat (1g sat. fat); 8g carbohydrates; 2g fiber; 3g sugars; 224mg sodium; 175mg calcium; 1.2mg iron; 547mg potassium; 49mg vitamin C; 6,637IU vitamin A

MEAT LOAF
WITH MASHED POTATOES

Since you cook the meat loaf and mashed potatoes at the same time in the multi-cooker, this is a true one-pot meal. If you can't find meat loaf mix, use 1 pound 80% lean ground beef and 1 pound lean ground pork.

· ·

1 In a food processor, pulse the oats until finely ground. Transfer to a large bowl. Combine the onion, celery, and garlic in the food processor and pulse until finely chopped.

2 Set the multi-cooker to Sauté and pour in the olive oil. When the oil is hot, add the chopped veggies and 1 teaspoon of the smoked paprika and cook, stirring, until the vegetables are soft, about 4 minutes. Press "Cancel." Transfer the veggies to the bowl with the oats and spread them out to cool slightly. Wipe out the pot with a paper towel, removing any veggie bits.

3 Add the meat loaf mix, egg, 2 teaspoons of the salt (if using), and the remaining 1 teaspoon paprika to the bowl with the vegetables and gently mix to combine. Place a large piece of aluminum foil on the counter and turn the meat mixture out on top. Form it into a loaf shape about 8 inches long and 2 inches high. Crimp the edges of the foil up around the loaf, leaving a little space around the edges.

4 Place the potatoes in the bottom of the multi-cooker. Sprinkle with the remaining ½ teaspoon salt (if using) and pour in the broth. Place the metal rack that came with the multi-cooker over the potatoes. Place the meat loaf on the foil on the rack. Lock the lid and set to cook on high pressure for 25 minutes. When cooking is complete, press "Cancel" and carefully quick-release the pressure.

(continues)

¾ cup rolled oats

1 small onion, quartered

1 celery stalk, cut into large pieces

2 garlic cloves

1 tablespoon olive oil

2 teaspoons smoked paprika

2 pounds meat loaf mix

1 large egg, lightly beaten

2½ teaspoons kosher salt (optional)

1½ pounds Yukon Gold potatoes, peeled and cut into 1-inch chunks

¾ cup low-sodium chicken broth

⅓ cup ketchup

4 teaspoons sherry vinegar

1 tablespoon unsalted butter

¼ cup whole milk

5 Set the oven to broil. In a small bowl, stir together the ketchup and vinegar. Wearing oven mitts, remove the meat loaf from the multi-cooker using the rack. Carefully tip any liquid out of the foil and discard it. Place the meatloaf in the foil on a baking sheet. Brush the top and sides of the meat loaf with the ketchup glaze. Broil the meat loaf until the glaze looks sticky and bubbles, 3 to 4 minutes. Let sit for at least 5 minutes before slicing.

6 Meanwhile, drain the potatoes and return them to the pot. Add the butter and milk and, using a potato masher, mash until creamy. Slice the meat loaf or cut it into baby-size bites and serve with the mashed potatoes.

Makes 6 servings

Nutrition per serving: 490 calories; 34g protein; 24g fat (9g sat. fat); 32g carbohydrates; 4g fiber; 5g sugars; 258mg sodium; 65mg calcium; 3.8mg iron; 1,023mg potassium; 24mg vitamin C; 222IU vitamin A

SAUSAGE RAGÙ ❄

Make this family-favorite sauce over the weekend for an easy dinner with pasta later in the week. Or divide it between into two containers and freeze one for instant supper insurance.

2 tablespoons olive oil

8 ounces sweet Italian sausage, casings removed if necessary

1 cup finely chopped fennel

One 28-ounce can whole tomatoes, crushed or coarsely chopped (see Note, page 167)

½ teaspoon kosher salt (optional)

2 tablespoons heavy cream

1 Set the multi-cooker to Sauté and pour in 1 tablespoon of the olive oil. When the oil is hot, add the sausage to the pot. Cook, stirring frequently, until browned and cooked through, about 5 minutes. Using a slotted spoon, transfer the sausage to a bowl.

2 Heat the remaining tablespoon olive oil in the cooker. Add the fennel and cook, stirring frequently, until very tender, about 10 minutes. If the pot gets too hot and the vegetables start to brown, add a little water.

3 Add the tomatoes with their juices and salt (if using). Lock the lid and set to cook on high pressure for 5 minutes.

4 When cooking is complete, press "Cancel" and carefully quick-release the pressure. Remove the lid and set the multi-cooker to Sauté. Return the sausage to the cooker and simmer for 5 minutes. Press "Cancel" and stir in the cream.

Makes 3½ cups

SLOW COOK IT: Double the recipe (except for the olive oil). Brown the Italian sausage in 2 tablespoons olive oil in a skillet on the stovetop. Add the fennel and cook for 2 minutes until beginning to soften. Transfer the mixture to a slow cooker. Add the tomatoes and salt (if using). Cover and cook on Low for 6 hours. Stir in the cream.

Nutrition per ½ cup serving: 119 calories; 6g protein; 8g fat (3g sat. fat); 6g carbohydrates; 2g fiber; 3g sugars; 336mg sodium; 49mg calcium; 2mg iron; 327mg potassium; 12mg vitamin C; 310IU vitamin A

SUMMER CORN SOUP

3 ears corn, shucked

2 tablespoons unsalted butter

1 leek, white and light green parts only, sliced (about 1 cup)

3 cups water

1 large russet potato, peeled and cubed

1 teaspoon kosher salt (optional)

1 sprig basil (optional)

¼ cup heavy cream

Freshly ground black pepper

Pretty please only make this soup when sweet corn is in season (that's roughly mid-July to mid-September in my neck of the woods). This soup is good hot, but even better refrigerated overnight and served chilled. The flavor is fuller, and the cold soup hits the spot on a hot summer's day.

1 Cut the kernels from the corncobs, reserving 2 cobs. Break the reserved cobs in half.

2 Set the multi-cooker to Sauté and melt the butter in the pot. Add the leek and cook, stirring frequently, until tender, about 5 minutes. If the leek starts to brown, add a little water to the pot.

3 Add the water, corn kernels, potato, corncob halves, salt (if using), and basil (if using). Lock the lid and set to cook on high pressure for 4 minutes.

4 When cooking is complete, press "Cancel" and carefully quick-release the pressure. Remove the lid and let the mixture cool slightly. Remove and discard the corncob halves and basil sprig. Using an immersion blender, blend until smooth. Stir in the cream and season with pepper. Serve warm, or refrigerate overnight and serve cold.

Makes 6 servings

Nutrition per serving: 185 calories; 4g protein; 8g fat (5g sat. fat); 28g carbohydrates; 3g fiber; 3g sugars; 17mg sodium; 23mg calcium; 1mg iron; 472mg potassium; 18mg vitamin C; 653IU vitamin A

ITALIAN-ISH ✋ ❄️
CHICKEN TENDERS

I learned the expression *"fare la scarpetta"* from my Italian in-laws. It literally means "make the little shoe," but refers to using bread to soak up the last bits of yummy sauce on your plate. This dish is the perfect opportunity to *fare la scarpetta*. So serve it with bread, and teach your little one some Italian over supper.

⅓ cup all-purpose flour

1 tablespoon Italian seasoning

1½ pounds chicken tenders

1¼ teaspoons kosher salt (optional)

3 to 4 tablespoons olive oil

1 red bell pepper, chopped

1 small onion, chopped

2 garlic cloves, thinly sliced

One 14-ounce can diced tomatoes

2 tablespoons heavy cream

Chopped fresh parsley and grated Parmesan cheese, for serving (optional)

1 Mix the flour and Italian seasoning together on a shallow dish. Season the chicken tenders with 1 teaspoon of the salt (if using). Dredge the chicken in the seasoned flour.

2 Set the multi-cooker to Sauté and pour in 1 tablespoon of the olive oil. When the oil is hot, working in two or three batches, add the chicken and brown for 2 to 3 minutes per side. Transfer each batch to a plate as you finish and repeat with the remaining chicken, using 1 tablespoon of oil per batch.

3 Heat the remaining 1 tablespoon oil in the pot. Add the bell pepper, onion, and remaining ¼ teaspoon salt (if using). Cook until tender, about 5 minutes. Add the garlic and cook for 1 minute more. Press "Cancel." Add the tomatoes with their juices and stir to combine, scraping up any browned bits from the bottom of the pot. Nestle the chicken into the sauce. Lock the lid and set to cook on high pressure for 8 minutes.

4 When cooking is complete, press "Cancel" and carefully quick-release the pressure. Transfer the chicken to a plate; cover with aluminum foil to keep warm.

(continues)

5 Set the multi-cooker to Sauté and let the sauce simmer for about 5 minutes to reduce it. Press "Cancel." Stir in the cream. Return the chicken to the sauce. Serve topped with grated Parmesan and parsley, if desired.

Makes 4 servings

· ·

Nutrition per serving: 351 calories; 41g protein; 14g fat (5g sat. fat); 14g carbohydrates; 3g fiber; 6g sugars; 281mg sodium; 40mg calcium; 1.5mg iron; 687mg potassium; 48mg vitamin C; 1,479IU vitamin A

MOROCCAN BRISKET

Brisket is an ideal cut of meat for pressure cooking. What would take hours in the oven becomes tender and succulent in half the time in your multi-cooker. Don't shy away from offering your baby olives—she just might surprise you and love them.

• •

1 In a small bowl, stir together the Moroccan seasoning, brown sugar (if using), salt (if using), and 2 tablespoons of the olive oil. Rub the spice mixture all over the brisket halves.

2 Set the multi-cooker to Sauté and pour in 1 tablespoon of the olive oil. When the oil is hot, brown 1 piece of brisket, about 4 minutes per side. Transfer the brisket half to a plate and repeat to brown the remaining brisket half.

3 Return the first brisket half to the cooker. Add the broth and water. Lock the lid and set to cook on high pressure for 80 minutes.

4 When cooking is complete, press "Cancel" and let the pressure release naturally. Transfer the brisket to a cutting board. Cover loosely with aluminum foil and let rest for 10 minutes.

5 In a small bowl, stir together the cilantro, lemon zest, olives, garlic, and remaining 2 tablespoons olive oil. Slice or shred the brisket, and serve it with the cilantro mixture alongside.

Makes 8 servings

(continues)

2 tablespoons Moroccan seasoning (also called ras el hanout)

2 tablespoons dark brown sugar (optional)

2 teaspoons kosher salt (optional)

5 tablespoons olive oil

One 4-pound brisket, halved

½ cup low-sodium beef broth

¼ cup water

1 cup chopped fresh cilantro

Zest of 1 lemon

¼ cup finely chopped pitted olives

1 garlic clove, finely chopped

SLOW COOK IT: Follow step 1 of the recipe as directed. Brown the brisket pieces in olive oil in a large skillet on the stovetop. Transfer the brisket to a 5- or 6-quart slow cooker. Add the broth and water. Cover and cook on Low until the meat is tender, about 8 hours. Proceed with step 5.

Nutrition per serving: 383 calories; 49g protein; 21g fat (5g sat. fat); 1g carbohydrates; 0g fiber; 0g sugars; 248mg sodium; 32mg calcium; 5mg iron; 837mg potassium; 2mg vitamin C; 149IU vitamin A

LAMB RAGÙ
WITH COUSCOUS

Trust me when I say to serve your baby's couscous stirred into the ragù. You'll thank me at cleanup time.

1 teaspoon ground cumin

Freshly ground black pepper

1¼ teaspoons kosher salt (optional)

1 pound boneless lamb stew meat, trimmed of fat and cut into 1-inch pieces

2 tablespoons olive oil

2 garlic cloves, sliced

One 28-ounce can whole tomatoes, chopped (see Note, page 167)

Pinch of sugar

One 10-ounce box plain instant couscous (such as Near East brand), prepared according to the package instructions

¼ cup chopped fresh cilantro

1 In a medium bowl, stir together the cumin, pepper, and 1 teaspoon of the salt (if using). Add the lamb and toss to coat.

2 Set the multi-cooker to Sauté and pour in 1 tablespoon of the olive oil. When the oil is hot, brown half the lamb, about 3 minutes per side. Transfer to a plate. Repeat with the remaining lamb, then transfer it to the plate with the first batch.

3 Heat the remaining 1 tablespoon olive oil in the pot. Add the garlic and cook for 1 minute. Add the tomatoes and their juices and scrape up any browned bits from the bottom of the pot.

4 Return the browned lamb to the pot and add the sugar and remaining ¼ teaspoon salt (if using). Lock the lid and set to cook on high pressure for 45 minutes.

5 When cooking is complete, press "Cancel" and let the pressure release naturally. Remove the lid and set the multi-cooker to Sauté. Simmer until the sauce has thickened, about 10 minutes.

6 Serve the ragù with couscous, garnished with the cilantro.

Makes 4 servings

SLOW COOK IT: Follow step 1 of the recipe as directed. In step 2, brown the meat in a large skillet on the stovetop. Transfer the lamb to a slow cooker along with the garlic, tomatoes, and sugar. Cover and cook on Low for 6 hours, or until tender. Serve as described in step 6.

Nutrition per serving: 528 calories; 34g protein; 13g fat (3g sat. fat); 62g carbohydrates; 5g fiber; 3g sugars; 97mg sodium; 36mg calcium; 4.4mg iron; 926mg potassium; 33mg vitamin C; 1,977IU vitamin A

BEEF, BEAN, AND ⊛ ❄
WHEAT BERRY CHILI

1 tablespoon plus 1 teaspoon canola oil

1 pound boneless beef stew meat, trimmed of fat and cut into 1-inch pieces

1¼ teaspoons kosher salt (optional)

1 red bell pepper, chopped

1 small onion, chopped

2 garlic cloves, minced

2 teaspoons chili powder

1½ cups cooked pinto beans, or one 15.5-ounce can, drained and rinsed

One 14.5-ounce can fire-roasted crushed tomatoes

¼ cup low-sodium beef broth

½ cup wheat berries

Optional toppings: grated cheddar cheese, chopped fresh cilantro, and sour cream

Wheat berries are a delightfully chewy whole grain. No, they're not traditional in chili, but they add heft, fiber, and texture. It might seem surprising, but chili is an excellent finger food. Serve baby's portion with only a little liquid, gently smash the beans, and make sure the meat is shredded or chopped into small pieces for your little eater.

• •

1 Set the multi-cooker to Sauté and pour in 1 tablespoon of the canola oil. Sprinkle the beef with ¾ teaspoon of the salt (if using) and add the meat to the pot. Cook, undisturbed, until beginning to brown, about 3 minutes. Flip and cook until lightly browned, about 3 minutes more. Transfer the meat to a plate.

2 Heat the remaining 1 teaspoon oil in the pot. Add the bell pepper, onion, garlic, remaining ½ teaspoon salt (if using), and the chili powder. Cook, stirring, until slightly softened, about 3 minutes. Add the beef and any juices that have collected on the plate, the beans, tomatoes, broth, and wheat berries. Lock the lid and set to cook on high pressure for 30 minutes.

3 When cooking is complete, press "Cancel" and carefully quick-release the pressure. Serve with the optional toppings, if desired.

Makes 4 servings

• •

Nutrition per serving: 412 calories; 35g protein; 11g fat (3g sat. fat); 45g carbohydrates; 12g fiber; 5g sugars; 368mg sodium; 54mg calcium; 4.5mg iron; 790mg potassium; 55mg vitamin C; 1,413IU vitamin A

BROCCOLI, SWISS, AND HAM STRATA

2 teaspoons unsalted butter, at room temperature

2 slices stale whole wheat bread, cut into 1-inch cubes

2 cups finely chopped broccoli florets with very little stem

2 ounces boiled ham, cut into ½-inch cubes (½ cup)

½ cup shredded Swiss cheese

4 large eggs

1½ cups whole milk

½ teaspoon kosher salt (optional)

Freshly ground black pepper

1½ cups water

If you don't have stale bread on hand, leave a couple of slices on a rack in the oven overnight.

1 Use the butter to grease a 1½-quart soufflé dish.

2 Layer half the bread, broccoli, ham, and cheese in the prepared dish. Repeat to make a second layer of each. In a large bowl, whisk together the eggs, milk, salt (if using), and several twists of pepper. Pour the egg mixture over the ingredients in the soufflé dish and gently press so all the ingredients are submerged in the liquid. Cover with aluminum foil and refrigerate for at least 1 hour or up to overnight.

3 Pour the water into the multi-cooker. Place the metal rack that came with the multi-cooker in the pot. Place the filled soufflé dish in a silicone or aluminum foil sling (see page 22). Lower the dish on the sling onto the rack. Lock the lid and set to cook on high pressure for 25 minutes.

4 Meanwhile, preheat the broiler. When cooking is complete, press "Cancel" and carefully quick-release the pressure. Using the sling, remove the soufflé dish from the multi-cooker and place it on a baking sheet. If there is any liquid on the surface of the strata, just dab it with a paper towel. Broil the strata for 2 to 3 minutes, until lightly golden brown. Let cool and serve.

Makes 4 servings

Nutrition per serving: 293 calories; 19g protein; 16g fat (8g sat. fat); 20g carbohydrates; 1g fiber; 6g sugars; 415mg sodium; 274mg calcium; 2.1mg iron; 319mg potassium; 34mg vitamin C; 1,619IU vitamin A

BUTTER CHICKEN ✋ ❄

Forget takeout—deliver this popular Indian dish to your table instead. Shredded chicken thighs are coated in a rich, buttery sauce with hints of tomatoes, ginger, and garam masala—a messy but very flavorful finger food.

1 Stir together the tomatoes, ginger, garlic, garam masala, and salt (if using) in the multi-cooker. Nestle the chicken into the tomato mixture. Lock the lid and set to cook on high pressure for 10 minutes.

2 When cooking is complete, press "Cancel" and let the pressure release naturally for 10 minutes, then carefully quick-release any remaining pressure. Transfer the chicken to a plate. Shred the meat with two forks. Cover with aluminum foil to keep warm.

3 Set the multi-cooker to Sauté. Once the sauce starts to bubble, stir in the butter until melted. Add the cream and simmer until the sauce has reduced slightly, about 2 minutes. Press "Cancel." Return the chicken to the sauce. Stir in the lime juice and serve garnished with cilantro.

Makes 4 servings

SLOW COOK IT: Stir together the tomatoes, ginger, garlic, garam masala, and salt (if using) in a slow cooker. Add the chicken. Cover and cook on Low for 6 to 8 hours, or until the chicken is tender and cooked through. Remove the chicken and shred it, then cover to keep warm. Transfer the sauce in the slow cooker to a medium pot and simmer on the stovetop until thickened. Stir in the shredded chicken and lime juice, and serve garnished with cilantro.

Nutrition per serving: 336 calories; 29g protein; 21g fat (10g sat. fat); 8g carbohydrates; 2g fiber; 3g sugars; 338mg sodium; 18mg calcium; 2.2mg iron; 317mg potassium; 15mg vitamin C; 867IU vitamin A

One 14-ounce can fire-roasted crushed tomatoes

1 tablespoon grated fresh ginger (from about a 1¼-inch piece)

2 garlic cloves, minced

1 teaspoon garam masala

1 teaspoon kosher salt (optional)

1 pound boneless, skinless chicken thighs, trimmed

2 tablespoons unsalted butter, cut into cubes

¼ cup heavy cream

1 teaspoon fresh lime juice

Chopped fresh cilantro, for garnish

BREAKFAST-FOR-DINNER
FRITTATA ✋ ❄️

Slice this veggie-packed sausage frittata into wedges for the family and cut it into bite-size pieces for your baby to self-feed. The frittata is superhot when it comes out of the oven, so make sure it has time to cool before serving.

• •

1 Set the multi-cooker to Sauté and pour in the olive oil. When the oil is hot, add the sausage to the pot. Cook, stirring frequently, until browned and cooked through, about 5 minutes. Add the spinach and stir until wilted. Use a slotted spoon to transfer the sausage and spinach to a bowl.

2 Using a paper towel, wipe out the pot. Pour 1½ cups water into the multi-cooker. Place the metal rack that came with the multi-cooker in the water.

3 Grease a 1½-quart round soufflé dish with the butter. Spread the butternut squash evenly in the dish. Top with the sausage-spinach mixture.

4 In a medium bowl, whisk together the eggs, milk, and salt (if using) and season with pepper. Pour the egg mixture over the squash and sausage in the soufflé dish. Place the dish in a silicone or aluminum foil sling (see page 22).

(continues)

1 tablespoon olive oil

4 ounces sweet Italian sausage, casings removed if necessary

2 cups packed baby spinach

1 teaspoon unsalted butter

2 cups diced peeled butternut squash (8 ounces, from 1 squash)

6 large eggs

½ cup whole milk

¾ teaspoon kosher salt (optional)

Freshly ground black pepper

¼ cup grated Parmesan cheese

5 Lower the dish on the sling onto the rack. Lock the lid and set to cook on high pressure for 25 minutes. When cooking is complete, press "Cancel" and let the pressure release naturally for 10 minutes, then carefully quick-release any remaining pressure. Use the sling to lift the dish out of the multi-cooker and set it on a baking sheet. Dab the top of the frittata dry with a paper towel.

6 Preheat the broiler. Sprinkle the frittata with the Parmesan. Broil until the cheese is melted and golden.

Makes 6 servings

· ·

Nutrition per serving: 182 calories; 13g protein; 11g fat (4g sat. fat); 8g carbohydrates; 1g fiber; 2g sugars; 267mg sodium; 133mg calcium; 2.1mg iron; 192mg potassium; 8mg vitamin C; 3,383IU vitamin A

EVERY BEAN SOUP ✋ ❄️

If you're an avid multi-cooker user, chances are you've got various partially empty bags of dried beans in your pantry. This is a super-simple recipe to use them up. Since you'll be cooking different varieties of beans, some of the quicker-cooking beans or split peas will become very soft and might even collapse into the broth (in a good way) in the time it takes for the longer-cooking varieties to soften. This soup is also delicious and nutritious for beginning eaters. Just purée it with an immersion blender right inside the pot. Or, to serve your baby's portion as a finger food, offer it with just a little broth and lightly smash the beans.

2 tablespoons olive oil

1 cup finely chopped onion

3 tablespoons tomato paste

6 cups water

2 cups dried beans (such as a mix of chickpeas, pinto beans, split peas, and cannellini beans), rinsed

1½ teaspoons kosher salt (optional)

1 teaspoon red wine vinegar

¼ cup finely chopped fresh parsley

Freshly ground black pepper

Olive oil, for serving (optional)

1 Set the multi-cooker to Sauté and pour in the olive oil. When the oil is hot, add the onion. Cook until soft, about 5 minutes. Add the tomato paste and stir to coat the onion. Press "Cancel."

2 Add the water, beans, and salt (if using). Lock the lid and set to cook on high pressure for 35 minutes if including chickpeas and/or cannellini beans or 30 minutes otherwise.

3 When cooking is complete, press "Cancel" and carefully quick-release the pressure. Stir in the vinegar and parsley. Season with pepper. Serve with a drizzle of olive oil, if desired.

Makes 6 servings

Nutrition per serving: 136 calories; 5g protein; 6g fat (1g sat. fat); 17g carbohydrates; 5g fiber; 4g sugars; 47mg sodium; 44mg calcium; 1.7mg iron; 219mg potassium; 7mg vitamin C; 269IU vitamin A

BEEF STROGANOFF ✋ ❄️

1 tablespoon plus 2 teaspoons olive oil

1 pound sirloin steak, cut into 2 x ¼-inch strips

1½ teaspoons kosher salt (optional)

1 small onion, chopped

2 garlic cloves, minced

8 ounces cremini or button mushrooms, trimmed and sliced ¼ inch thick

½ teaspoon Worcestershire sauce

¼ cup plus 1 tablespoon low-sodium beef broth

1 tablespoon all-purpose flour

¼ cup plain full-fat Greek yogurt

1 tablespoon Dijon mustard

2 tablespoons chopped fresh parsley

Serve this meaty meal with egg noodles; cut your baby's egg noodles into small pieces before serving.

· ·

1 Set the multi-cooker to Sauté and pour in 1 tablespoon of the olive oil. Season the beef with 1 teaspoon of the salt (if using). Add half the beef and cook, undisturbed, until light brown on the bottom, 3 minutes. Flip and cook until light brown on the second side, 2 to 3 minutes. Using a slotted spoon, transfer the beef to a plate. Repeat with another 1 teaspoon of the oil to cook the remaining beef, then transfer the meat to the plate.

2 Heat the remaining 1 teaspoon oil in the pot. Add the onion, garlic, mushrooms, and remaining ½ teaspoon salt (if using) and cook, stirring, until soft, about 3 minutes. Press "Cancel." Stir in the Worcestershire and ¼ cup of the broth, scraping up any browned bits on the bottom of the pot. Return the beef and any juices to the pot. Lock the lid and set to cook on high pressure for 18 minutes.

3 When cooking is complete, press "Cancel" and let the pressure release naturally for 10 minutes, then carefully quick-release any remaining pressure. Remove the lid. Set the multi-cooker to Sauté. In a small bowl, stir together the flour and remaining 1 tablespoon broth. Once the liquid in the multi-cooker is simmering, stir in the flour-broth mixture and cook, stirring, until slightly thickened, 1 to 2 minutes. Press "Cancel." Stir in the yogurt, mustard, and parsley and serve.

Makes 4 servings

· ·

Nutrition per serving: 248 calories; 29g protein; 11g fat (3g sat. fat); 6g carbohydrates; 1g fiber; 3g sugars; 181mg sodium; 57mg calcium; 2.4mg iron; 640mg potassium; 5mg vitamin C; 171IU vitamin A

VERY VEGGIE SOUP ❄

Like risotto, this comforting soup is a particularly good one for babies to practice self-feeding with a spoon, since it's thick enough that it won't all drip off the utensil.

1 Set the multi-cooker to Sauté and pour in the olive oil. When the oil is hot, add the onion, cauliflower, carrots, cumin seeds, and ½ teaspoon of the salt (if using). Cook, stirring frequently, for 10 minutes, letting the vegetables soften and brown a bit.

2 Pour the water or broth into the multi-cooker. Add the squash. Lock the lid and set to cook on high pressure for 5 minutes.

3 When cooking is complete, press "Cancel" and carefully quick-release the pressure. Remove the lid and let the mixture cool slightly. Blend with an immersion blender or in a standard blender (take care when blending hot foods; see page 59). Stir in the cheese, remaining ¼ teaspoon salt (if using), and a big squeeze of lemon juice. Serve topped with a drizzle of olive oil, some pepper, and a little flaky sea salt, if desired.

Makes 6 servings

SLOW COOK IT: Omit the olive oil and cumin seeds. Combine the onion, cauliflower, carrots, salt (if using), broth, and squash in a slow cooker. Cover and cook on Low for 5 to 6 hours, or until the vegetables are tender. Proceed with step 3.

¼ cup olive oil

1 cup chopped onion

4 cups cauliflower florets (from 1 head)

4 carrots, peeled and chopped

1 teaspoon cumin seeds

¾ teaspoon kosher salt (optional)

2 cups water or low-sodium vegetable broth

2 cups chopped peeled butternut squash (about 10 ounces, from 1 squash)

½ cup shredded provolone, Gruyère, or cheddar cheese (1 ounce)

1 lemon wedge

Olive oil, freshly ground black pepper, and flaky sea salt, for serving (optional)

Nutrition per serving: 170 calories; 4g protein; 11g fat (2g sat. fat); 17g carbohydrates; 4g fiber; 6g sugars; 140mg sodium; 104mg calcium; 1.3mg iron; 550mg potassium; 47mg vitamin C; 11,797IU vitamin A

TOMATO SOUP ❄
WITH PARMESAN TOAST TRIANGLES

2 tablespoons olive oil

1 cup chopped onion

1 garlic clove, chopped

½ teaspoon fennel seeds

1 cup water

One 28-ounce can diced tomatoes

½ teaspoon kosher salt (optional)

3 slices whole-wheat sandwich bread

1 teaspoon balsamic vinegar

2 tablespoons grated Parmesan cheese

Whole-wheat sandwich bread does double-duty here, thickening the soup and serving as the base for easy, cheesy dippers.

1 Set the multi-cooker to Sauté and pour in the olive oil. When the oil is hot, add the onion. Cook, stirring frequently, until the onion is soft, about 5 minutes. Add the garlic and fennel seeds and cook for 1 minute more.

2 Pour the water into the multi-cooker. Add the tomatoes and salt (if using). Tear one piece of bread into pieces and stir it into the soup mixture. Lock the lid and set to cook on high pressure for 3 minutes.

3 When cooking is complete, press "Cancel" and carefully quick-release the pressure. Remove the lid and let the mixture cool slightly. Blend with an immersion blender or in an upright blender (take care when blending hot foods; see page 59). Stir in the vinegar.

4 Preheat the broiler. Line a sheet pan with aluminum foil. Toast the remaining 2 slices bread in a toaster. Place the toasted bread on the prepared baking sheet. Sprinkle each slice with 1 tablespoon of the Parmesan. Broil until the cheese is melted and golden, about 2 minutes. Cut the toast into triangles and serve them with the soup.

Makes 4 servings

Nutrition per serving: 184 calories; 6g protein; 8g fat (2g sat. fat); 23g carbohydrates; 5g fiber; 9g sugars; 530mg sodium; 104mg calcium; 1.3mg iron; 124mg potassium; 17mg vitamin C; 816IU vitamin A

VEGGIE TOFU NOODLE SOUP

Serve your baby's portion with just a little bit of broth so it's more finger food than soup. You can also serve it as a mixed dish or separate out the components.

1 Place the onions, carrots, celery, garlic, ginger, star anise (if using), bay leaf, water, and salt (if using) in the multi-cooker. Lock the lid and set to cook on high pressure for 20 minutes.

2 Meanwhile, line a plate with paper towels, put the tofu on the plate, and cover with more paper towels. Place another plate on top, then top that with a heavy can or pot to press the tofu and remove the liquid.

3 When cooking is complete, press "Cancel" and carefully quick-release the pressure. Using a slotted spoon, remove and discard the solids in the broth. (It's okay if a few pieces remain.) Add the mushrooms, noodles, and spinach, pressing them down to submerge them in the liquid (they won't all be covered—that's okay). Reseal the pot and set to cook on high pressure for 1 minute. (It will take a few minutes for the contents of the pot to cool down enough for you to reseal the lid.)

4 When cooking is complete, press "Cancel" and let the pressure release naturally for 10 minutes, then carefully quick-release any remaining pressure. Stir in the fish sauce (if using).

5 Cut the pressed tofu into ½-inch cubes. Serve the soup with the tofu, some cilantro, and lime wedges for squeezing.

Makes 4 servings

Nutrition per serving: 283 calories; 10g protein; 6g fat (0g sat. fat); 47g carbohydrates; 4g fiber; 6g sugars; 311mg sodium; 237mg calcium; 3.1mg iron; 94mg potassium; 63mg vitamin C; 4,169IU vitamin A

3 small onions, cut into wedges

3 carrots, peeled and chopped

3 celery stalks, chopped

3 garlic cloves, sliced

One 1-inch piece fresh ginger, sliced into coins (no need to peel it)

2 star anise pods (optional)

1 bay leaf

5 cups water

½ teaspoon kosher salt (optional)

8 ounces firm tofu

1 cup sliced shiitake mushroom caps

6 ounces flat rice noodles (stir-fry noodles)

5 ounces baby spinach

1½ teaspoons fish sauce (optional)

Chopped fresh cilantro and lime wedges, for serving

LEMON-DILL 🖐 ⏱ SALMON

½ cup low-sodium chicken broth or water

1 tablespoon Dijon mustard

Four 4-ounce center-cut skin-on salmon fillets, 1 to 1¾ inches thick, any bones removed

Pinch of kosher salt (optional)

1 tablespoon unsalted butter

1 tablespoon chopped fresh dill

1 tablespoon fresh lemon juice

It's hard to overcook fish in the multi-cooker; fillets are almost effortlessly moist and tender. Keep this nutritious salmon dish in your regular repertoire to help ensure that your baby gets plenty of the omega-3s her developing brain craves. Flake the salmon with a fork before serving it to your baby.

• •

1 Whisk together the broth and mustard in a multi-cooker. Place the metal rack that came with the multi-cooker in the pot. Sprinkle the salmon with the salt (if using). Place the fillets skin-side down on the rack, not touching one another, if possible. Lock the lid and set to cook on low pressure for 2 minutes.

2 When cooking is complete, press "Cancel" and let the pressure naturally release for 5 minutes. (Even if the float valve lowers before 5 minutes is up, let the salmon sit for the entire time.)

3 Transfer the rack with the salmon to a plate and cover with aluminum foil. Set the multi-cooker to Sauté and bring the cooking liquid to a simmer. Whisk in the butter and simmer the sauce until slightly thickened and reduced, about 2 minutes. Press "Cancel." Stir in the dill and lemon juice. Serve the salmon topped with the sauce.

Makes 4 servings

• •

Nutrition per serving: 192 calories; 23g protein; 10g fat (3g sat. fat); 1g carbohydrates; 0g fiber; 0g sugars; 149mg sodium; 15mg calcium; 1mg iron; 561mg potassium; 2mg vitamin C; 145IU vitamin A

BEANS, GREENS, AND PASTA

Broccoli rabe, a.k.a. rapini, is one bitter vegetable. Tempered with a sprinkle of sea salt and a squeeze of lemon juice, I love it, and so does my kid. This hearty dish is a great way to introduce your baby to this challenging green. But if broccoli rabe is a no-go for your little one or for other members of your family, skip it and stir in a 5-ounce package of baby spinach after the beans and pasta have finished cooking.

2 tablespoons olive oil, plus more for drizzling

3 garlic cloves, sliced

1 cup dried great northern beans, rinsed

3 cups water

1¼ teaspoons kosher salt (optional)

½ pound broccoli rabe (about ½ bunch), tough stems removed, chopped

½ cup ditalini or other small pasta

Lemon zest, grated Parmesan cheese, and freshly ground black pepper, for serving (optional)

1 Set the multi-cooker to Sauté and pour in the olive oil. Add the garlic and cook, stirring frequently, for 1 minute.

2 Add the beans, water, and salt (if using). Lock the lid and set to cook on high pressure for 30 minutes.

3 When cooking is complete, press "Cancel" and carefully quick-release the pressure. Add the broccoli rabe and pasta to the pot. Lock the lid again and set to cook on high pressure for 3 minutes.

4 When cooking is complete, press "Cancel" and carefully quick-release the pressure. Stir for a minute or two before serving. Serve topped with a drizzle of olive oil, some lemon zest, Parmesan, and/or pepper, if desired.

Makes 4 servings

Nutrition per serving: 297 calories; 15g protein; 8g fat (1g sat. fat); 44g carbohydrates; 10g fiber; 2g sugars; 30mg sodium; 126mg calcium; 4mg iron; 728mg potassium; 55mg vitamin C; 3,667IU vitamin A

acknowledgments

Writing this section is always my favorite part of the cookbook-creation process. I so enjoy having the chance to express my gratitude to all the wonderful people in my life—in print!

As always, thank you to Sharon Bowers, my agent and friend, whose professional and personal support are so meaningful to me.

Thank you to the marvelous team at HMH, first and foremost Stephanie Fletcher, my editor extraordinaire. Your insight makes everything I write better. Brianna Yamashita, Samantha Trovillion, Sari Kamin, and Bridget Nocera, thank you for your tireless efforts to spread the word. And a special shout-out to Alissa Faden and Melissa Lotfy. Your design talents truly make this book and my others stand out in a crowd.

And what can I say about the best photo team in the biz? Lauren Volo, Monica Pierini, and Maeve Sheridan—you made beautiful, delightful images that I am so excited to share far and wide.

Toby Amidor, thank you for your deep nutrition knowledge, helpful advice, and utter professionalism. Liz Tarpy, thank you for your recipe testing help; you were a lifesaver!

A huge thank-you goes to my brilliant colleagues at *Parents* and *Health* magazines. It is a thrill to come to work every day to collaborate with such kind and talented teams. I still pinch myself that it is actually my job to think about food all day. Thank you also to Steve Engel, Heidi Reavis, and all of my friends at Engel Entertainment.

Danielle Wilkie, Allison Graham, Felicity Rowe, Nicole Page, Jessica Winchell Morsa, and Grace Bastidas, your friendship makes my life complete.

To my parents, Andy and Linda Helwig: thank you, and I love you. It was all-hands-on-deck this past year, and understanding that I could count on you made a world of difference.

To Rosen, my heart lives in your body. Knowing that other parents feel the same fierce love for their children inspires me when I write these books.

And, last but not least, to my funny, caring, cheerleader of a husband. Dave, you make everything possible. Every year that passes further confirms how truly fortunate I am to share my life with you.

INDEX

Note: Page references in *italics*
indicate photographs.

T

V

W

Walnut Butter, DIY, 134, *134*
Water, 169
Wheat Berry, Beef, and Bean Chili, 192, *193*

Y

Yogurt, Greek-Style, 78–79

Z

Zinc, 32, 33
Zucchini
    Chicken and Veg Stew, 174, *175*
    Greek Meatball Pitas, 152, *153*
    Rapid Ratatouille, *94*, 95
    Squash and Pepper Purée, 99
    and Summer Squash Purée, 80

METRIC CONVERSION GUIDE

Note: The recipes in this cookbook have not
been developed or tested using metric measures.
When converting recipes to metric,
some variations in quality may be noted.

Measurements

INCHES	CENTIMETERS
1	2.5
2	5.0
3	7.5
4	10.0
5	12.5
6	15.0
7	17.5
8	20.5
9	23.0
10	25.5
11	28.0
12	30.5
13	33.0

Temperatures

FAHRENHEIT	CELSIUS
32°	0°
212°	100°
250°	120°
275°	140°
300°	150°
325°	160°
350°	180°
375°	190°
400°	200°
425°	220°
450°	230°
475°	240°
500°	260°

Volume

U.S. UNITS	CANADIAN METRIC	AUSTRALIAN METRIC
¼ teaspoon	1 mL	1 ml
½ teaspoon	2 mL	2 ml
1 teaspoon	5 mL	5 ml
1 tablespoon	15 mL	20 ml
¼ cup	50 mL	60 ml
⅓ cup	75 mL	80 ml
½ cup	125 mL	125 ml
⅔ cup	150 mL	170 ml
¾ cup	175 mL	190 ml
1 cup	250 mL	250 ml
1 quart	1 liter	1 liter
1½ quarts	1.5 liters	1.5 liters
2 quarts	2 liters	2 liters
2½ quarts	2.5 liters	2.5 liters
3 quarts	3 liters	3 liters
4 quarts	4 liters	4 liters

Weight

U.S. UNITS	CANADIAN METRIC	AUSTRALIAN METRIC
1 ounce	30grams	30 grams
2 ounces	55 grams	60 grams
3 ounces	85 grams	90 grams
4 ounces (¼ pound)	115 grams	125 grams
8 ounces	225 grams	225 grams
16 ounces (1 pound)	455 grams	500 grams
1 pound	455 grams	0.5 kilogram